THE HISTORY

OF

WEED

IN

101 OBJECTS

Media Lab Books

For inquiries, call 646-838-6637

Copyright 2017 Topix Media Lab

Published by Topix Media Lab
14 Wall Street, Suite 4B, New York, NY 10005

Printed in China

ISBN-10: 1-942556-63-2
ISBN-13: 978-1-942556-63-3

CEO **Tony Romando**

VICE PRESIDENT OF BRAND MARKETING **Joy Bomba**
DIRECTOR OF FINANCE **Vandana Patel**
DIRECTOR OF SALES AND NEW MARKETS **Tom Mifsud**
MANUFACTURING DIRECTOR **Nancy Puskuldjian**
FINANCIAL ANALYST **Matthew Quinn**
BRAND MARKETING ASSISTANT **Taylor Hamilton**

EDITOR-IN-CHIEF **Jeff Ashworth**
CREATIVE DIRECTOR **Steven Charny**
PHOTO DIRECTOR **Dave Weiss**
MANAGING EDITOR **Courtney Kerrigan**
SENIOR EDITOR **James Ellis**

CONTENT EDITOR **Tim Baker**
CONTENT DESIGNER **Michelle Lock**
CONTENT PHOTO EDITOR **Catherine Armanasco**
ART DIRECTOR **Susan Dazzo**
ASSOCIATE ART DIRECTOR **Rebecca Stone**
ASSISTANT MANAGING EDITOR **Holland Baker**
DESIGNER **Danielle Santucci**
ASSISTANT PHOTO EDITOR **Jessica Ariel Wendroff**
ASSISTANT EDITORS **Trevor Courneen, Alicia Kort, Kaytie Norman**
EDITORIAL ASSISTANT **Isabella Torchia**

CO-FOUNDERS **Bob Lee, Tony Romando**

FOR CENTURIES, the flowers, stalks, leaves, seeds and fibers of cannabis have been used by civilizations around the world for purposes from making clothing to creating cookery to, yes, getting high. From the first chillum to ever gobsmack an ancient Indian priest to the perfectly crafted joints sold at dispensaries in the 21st century, cannabis has been a part of human culture that, try though some might, has never been eradicated or had its use stifled. In the following pages, we offer the story of humankind's relationship with this incredible plant through 101 vital objects from our shared history. Whether it's the Zig-Zag papers that roll up your weed or the Twinkie you reach for after you've smoked it, we've left no stone unturned.

SCYTHIAN TOMBS

THROUGHOUT ANCIENT and medieval history, the nomadic horsemen of near and east Asia were among the most feared conquerors, from the Huns to Genghis Khan to the Golden Horde. But the first of these peoples to conquer vast portions of the world's largest contiguous land mass were the Scythians. Riding out from the grasslands of Eurasia to create havoc for Greek and Persian settlements and city-states in the second millennium B.C., the Scythians were fierce warriors, and, as recent archaeological evidence has uncovered, among history's first widespread cannabis users. The plant can be found, in addition to opium in more westerly sites, in tombs of important Scythians along with its burned residue, suggesting toking up was an important part of Scythian ritual.

שמבונין הן אבותם ליורד לבוא אומרים
לפניו רבונו של עולם מאחר שאתה עתיד
ליפרע מהן למה הקדמתה שנידם כם אמר
ר' אילעא בר יברכיה אלמלא תפלתו של
דוד היו כל ישראל מוכרי רבב שנאמר
שירה ה' מורה להם וא"ר אילעא בר
יברכיה אלמלא תפלתו של חבקוק היו ב'
תלמידי חכמים מתכסים בטלית אחת ועוסקין
בתורה שנאמר ה' שמעתי שמעך יראתי
ה' פעלך בקרב שנים חייהו אל תקרא בקרב
שנים אלא בקרוב שנים ואמר ר' אילעא
בר יברכיה שני תלמידי חכמים המהלכין
בדרך ואין ביניהן דברי תורה ראוין לישרף
באש שנאמר ויהי המה הולכים הלוך ודבר
והנה רכב אש וגו' טעמא דאיכא דיבור
הא ליכא דיבור ראוין לישרף וא"ר אילעא
בר יברכיה שני ת"ח הדרין בעיר אחת ואין
נוחין זה לזה בהלכה אחד מת ואחד גולה
שנאמר לנוס שמה רוצח אשר ירצח את
רעהו בבלי דעת ואין דעת אלא תורה
שנאמר נדמו עמי מבלי הדעת אמר ר'
יהודה בריה דר' חייא כל ת"ח העוסק
בתורה מתוך הדחק תפלתו נשמעת שנאמר
כי עם בציון ישב בירושלים בכה לא תבכה
חנון יחנך לקול זעקך כשמעתו ענך וכתיב
בתריה ונתן (ה) ה' לכם לחם צר ומים לחץ
ר' אבהו אומר משביעין אותו מזיו שכינה
שנאמר והיו עיניך רואות את מוריך ר'
אחא בר חנינא אמר אף אין הפרגוד ננעל
בפניו שנאמר ולא יכנף עוד מוריך: רשב"ג
אומר משום ר' יהושע מיום שחרב בהמ"ק
אין וכו': אמר רבא בכל יום ויום מרובה
קללתו משל חבירו שנאמר בבקר תאמר
מי יתן ערב ובערב תאמר מי יתן בקר הי
בקר אילימא בקר דלמחר מי ידע מאי הוי
אלא דחליף ואלא עלמא אמאי קא מקיים
אקדושה דסידרא ואיהא שמיה רבא דאגדתא
שנא' ארץ עפתה כמו אופל צלמות ולא
סדרים הא יש סדרים תופיע מאופל: ולא
ירד טל לברכה וניטל טעם פירות וכו':
תניא ר"ש בן אלעזר אומר טהרה בטלה
טעם וריח מעשר ביטל שומן דגן רב הונא
אשכח תומרתא דחינוניתא שקלה כרכה
בסודריה אתא רבה בריה א"ל מורחנא ריחא
דחינוניתא א"ל בני טהרה יש בך יהבה
ניהליה אדהכי אתא אבא בריה שקלה יהבה
ניהליה א"ל בני שמחת את לבי והקהית את
שיני והיינו דאמרי אינשי רחמי דאבא אבני

[illegible]

מתני'

[illegible]

נתנו עיניהם בשמואל הקטן וכשמת הספידוהו
ת מיתתו שמעון וישמעאל לחרבא וחברוהי
גמא ואף על ר' יהודה בן בבא בקשו לומר
זוגי מלכות: משחרב בהמ"ק בטל השמיר
בהבנותו אבן שלמה מסע נבנה הדברים
ן והלא כבר נאמר כל אלה אבנים יקרות
נותו שהיה מתקין מבחוץ ומכניס מבפנים
יה באבני ביתו ור' נחמיה שמיר למאי אתא
ום שנאמר פתוחי חותם ואין משרטין עליהם
ראה להן שמיר מבחוץ והן נבקעות מאליהן
זו שנבקעת בימות הגשמים ואינה חסרה
רא ואין כל דבר קשה יכול לעמוד בפניו
באיטני של אבר מליאה סובי שעורין אמר
בנה תניא נמי הכי משחרב מקדש ראשון
דוש הבא משגיר הדומה כעיגולי דבילה:

[illegible]

THE TALMUD

"Then the Lord said to Moses, "Take the following fine spices: 500 shekels of liquid myrrh, half as much of fragrant cinnamon, 250 shekels of kaneh-bosm, 500 shekels of cassia...and a hind of olive oil. Make these into a sacred anointing oil."
— *Exodus 30:23*

WITHIN THESE instructions to make Holy Oil, researchers and religious scholars agree that the ingredient "Kaneh-Bosm," found in several passages of the Talmud, most likely translates to cannabis. Dr. Yosef Glassman of the New England Sinai Hospital in Massachusetts has also proposed the sacred mixture wasn't just used ritually to anoint skin, but also as incense during times of turmoil. As commanded by God in Exodus 30:8–10, this incense was burned daily in tents by Moses's brother Aaron, the High Priest of Israel. As a consequence, cannabis as a sacred healing plant was prominent in the everyday life of Ancient Israelis. Additionally, in the Israeli newspaper *Haaretz*, Glassman revealed another discovery: Cannabis was probably used as an anesthetic by Ancient Israelites as well. A dig find in the city of Beit Shemesh uncovered hashish in the stomach of the 1,623-year-old remains of a 14-year-old girl who had died in childbirth, revealing cannabis was a valued part of medical tradition in Judaism thousands of years ago.

MUMMY OF RAMSES II

THE ROLE OF CANNABIS in ancient Egypt is still a complicated one for Egyptologists to understand. While we have proof the plant existed and was used for various purposes, this proof gives us no idea of the breadth of cultivation and methods of use. The mummies of pharaohs Akhenaten (also known as Amenhotep IV), which was found partly bound with hempen rope, and Ramses II, who has a considerable amount of hemp pollen coating his wraps, prove that cannabis existed in Egypt at the time of his death in 1213 B.C. But this is all the concrete proof there is, according to *Cannabis: A History* by Martin Booth. Booth's text notes that while some scholars link an Egyptian character used to connote a salve, sedative and cure for glaucoma to hemp, this connection cannot be definitively proven.

HEMP ROPE AND CLOTH

WHILE FULL-SCALE industrial cultivation of hemp wouldn't be used until c. 2800 B.C. in China, remains of hempen ropes used for a variety of purposes—as well as of hempen garments—have been found in Mesopotamian archaeological dig sites thought to be 8,000 years old. The use of hemp rope and cloth wouldn't reach Europe for millennia, but the beginning of hemp's utility beyond its flowers began in the cradle of civilization itself. As industrial capability expanded, so did the breadth of hemp production around the world. In many ways, the plant would reach its full potential industrially in the U.S. during World War II, when the U.S. government eased prohibitions on growing hemp due to the plant's usefulness in multiple war efforts, from textiles for uniforms to twine and paper for packaging. Today, industrial hemp remains one of the most lucrative cash crops in countries and states that allow its cultivation. The market for hemp rope necklaces has dipped, however.

承蒙　閣
好　下允諾　介紹學生
感情之至　現時期
該學生已將　諸
概料理齊備　鑒昨接
定于是月初
行李衣服一
十月送到
實請學習時
意務乙
閣下隨時
激訓使其可
成業將來
水不忘
台安敬
肅此奉陳敬
某某仁兄賜
來校

●介紹學生

橋　金　雲　系　鵲　翦　石　香鳫
寺　寺　寺　寺　寺　寺　寺　　去　痙病萬蛋
奇　皆　該　挨　猜　樏　筐　搌　眵目
開　也　也　推　怪　拉　師　弱上　盞屬
　　　　　　　　又　　　　　　　也　又屬
寺　蚧　鰓　採　腮　揷　攐　也八
乘　屈　戒　彩　鰥　彩　肜　膔去
　　糖　誡　饟　緑　崖　　　瀝灑
寺　　　　案　　水　　　曬乾
開　鮡　堦　呃　涯　埦　醸　灑
　　　界　街　崖　堆　酒　洒汎
寺　街　堦　岌　推　唾　瀝　殼
慨　四通　割　根　矮　沬　減也
　　　　　　　睡　　界　
寺　塜　尬　改　睡　　　　士晨
凱　堦　价　溉　唲　　　老也
懲　　　　滌　睉　　　微弱
鎧　怪　解　雊　
　垔　欻　槼　斗平

THE WORLD'S FIRST PAPER

AS FAR AS our current archaeological records can tell, the earliest civilization to cultivate hemp for industrial purposes was ancient China. According to the September/October 2000 edition of MIT's journal *The Thistle*, the Chinese have been cultivating cannabis for 6,000 continuous years. The next cultivator in the Old World was France, which has been producing hemp for only 700 years. The most important innovation the ancient Chinese were able to create using hemp was, by far, paper. While Europeans were still writing on animal skins and cultures all over the world used hammered reed sheets, bones and whatever else was available, Chinese artisans had perfected the first modern paper product—entirely from hemp.

BAJA HOODIE

A CELEBRATED PIECE of the stereotypical stoner uniform, the Baja Hoodie is a poncho-like pullover often associated with hippie and cannabis culture. Though today they are colloquially referred to as "drug rugs," the woven shirts were first called "sudadera de jerga." Traditionally fashioned after blankets, they were popularized in Mexico. In the 1970s, surfers from California began bringing these sweaters back from their surf trips in Baja California, Mexico. The striped pullovers quickly became synonymous with the West Coast hippie, and by the '80s, stoners depicted in mainstream film or TV—such as Sean Penn's Jeff Spicoli in *Fast Times at Ridgemont High*—were often sporting Baja hoodies. Despite the hoodie being a time-honored symbol of counterculture, high fashion brands have recently tried to emulate the sweater's laid-back design. In 2014, Michael Kors sold a $1,150 silk Baja Hoodie, and an Alexander Wang version once retailed for $1,895.

7

HEMP CLOTHES

HEMP'S POSSIBILITY for clothing and its industrial production are well-established and have been for thousands of years, but 21st century ingenuity is making the possibilities of hemp even more pronounced. As a plant of which almost every part is useful and profitable, hemp has found a new-age home with American made Jungmaven, which makes an extensive series of clothing, bath products, rope twine and composites—all from hemp. Since February 2013, Colorado-based EnviroTextiles has been the only hemp-based manufacturer to qualify to list their products in the USDA's Federal Procurement Preferred category. Aiming for complete sustainability, products like those created by Jungmaven might be the key to proving cannabis's market potential in the green age.

W. B. O'SHAUGHNESSY'S RESEARCH

KNOWN IN MEDICAL and in cannabis enthusiast
circles as the father of western medical cannabis, the
Irishman W. B. O'Shaughnessy was born poor in
Limerick in 1809 and was accepted as a prodigy to the
University of Edinburgh's medical school at just 18.
By the time he was 30 years old, he had revolutionized
treatment of cholera and written the first medical
defense of cannabis, a 40-page treatise which traced the
history of cannabis's use in ancient India and Persia to
the plant's more modern potential. He began to prepare
tinctures and give them to patients suffering from
rheumatism, hydrophobia, cholera and tetanus, as well
as a 40-day-old baby with convulsions who went from
"near-death" to "the enjoyment of robust health."

9

BLOWN GLASS

THOUGH IT'S CURRENTLY one of the simplest methods of smoking pot, the glass pipe's origins have a long and complex history dating back to 1500 B.C. The practice of glass making has roots in Egypt and Mesopotamia, where glass was molded from molten sand. The process was lengthy and difficult until around the first century A.D. when glassblowing emerged in Rome. Blowing into the glass when warmed allowed it to be formed more easily and with greater control—making way for the creation of everyday objects such as drinking glasses, plates and mirrors. Later, the Middle Ages saw a revitalization of glassblowing by Venetian glassworkers in Murano, which eventually led to the creation of more decorative and colorful glass works.

Glass pipes are made with this same glassblowing technique—and the emergence is often attributed to artist Bob Snodgrass, who made pipes as he followed the Grateful Dead on tour in the '80s. He eventually began teaching the technique in 1990, and many of his students opened shops of their own as the glass pipes grew in popularity. Tommy Chong further pushed glass into the cannabis spotlight with his own line of pipes and "Chong Bongs"—he'd eventually be given a nine-month prison sentence for selling "drug paraphernalia" in 2003 after federal agents targeted his online business in a series of raids focused on large internet weed distributors.

10

HOOKAH

The Caterpillar and Alice looked at each other for some time in silence: At last the Caterpillar took the hookah out of its mouth, and addressed her in a languid, sleepy voice… "Who are YOU?" said the Caterpillar.
—**Alice's Adventures in Wonderland**
by Lewis Carroll

ORIGINATING in the 16th century, the hookah came into being when the British East India Trading Company began exporting glass to India. The first hookahs, while primitive in their glass design, were used to smoke opium and hashish. They gained popularity further west during the Ottoman Empire's rule around 1600 when the Turks were introduced to tobacco from Europe—quickly making it the favored substance to smoke at social gatherings. As hookahs became larger and more intricate in design, shape and color, they also began serving as status symbols for intellectuals and the upper class in 17th century Turkey.

One of the first appearances of the hookah in the Western world surfaced in *Alice's Adventures in Wonderland* in 1865. However, hookah didn't enter into mainstream American culture until the mid-1960s. With cannabis integrated into the hippie lifestyle, many college students turned to the hookah when smoking in groups, choosing to mix hash with tobacco as an alternative to a joint or pipe and create a more communal smoking experience.

ZIG-ZAG ROLLING PAPER

THE IDEA OF rolling up one's smoke in paper may have first come to a frustrated cigarette smoker during the Crimean War, but in the 20th and 21st centuries, the famous brand of papers that bears this intrepid soldier's face, Zig-Zag, is more associated with cannabis than tobacco. Or, as Afro Man popularly puts it, "Colt 45 and two Zig-Zags/Baby that's all we need/We could go to the park, after dark/And smoke that tumbleweed." "The Zouave," as the mascot on the Zig-Zag wrapper is known, is the avatar of a specially trained infantry regiment from the French Army who, having broken his pipe during the Battle of Sevastopol, rolled the first cigarette using paper from his ammunition box. The Zouave, with his trademark beard and fez, is now the unofficial mascot of pot smokers who prefer their joints to have a little more historical significance than the leading brand.

12

HOMEMADE APPLE PIPE

FOR THE LOYAL FRIEND of clandestine smokers who don't want to buy permanent fixtures, MacGyver-style smokers who feel a special frisson while DIY-smoking and anyone who's really into composting, homemade apple pipes have made nick-of-time saves more often than World Cup goalkeepers. No one knows exactly which enterprising smoker first figured it out, but apple pipes have become as American as apple pie since gaining popularity in the 1960s. With nothing but an apple and a pen, cannabis enthusiasts in need can simply bore three holes in the apple—one after removing the stem in the top, the bowl; one near the bottom, the carb; and one in the side, the mouthpiece. Just please, please don't eat the apple after.

BLUNT

"Now Johnny's cool
He knows where it's at
Smoking good blunts..."
—Just-Ice, "Little Bad Johnny"

THE DESCENDANT OF the traditional Jamaican fronto leaf, with which cannabis was rolled into a cigar-shape, the blunt is the go-to smoking apparatus of those for whom a joint is too small, a bowl isn't communal enough and anything more elaborate is just affectation. Hip-hop legend says that the first recorded use of the word blunt to describe a hollowed-out cigar leaf filled with cannabis occurred when rapper Just-Ice dropped the song "Little Bad Johnny." Since this 1986 genesis, blunts have become so ubiquitous that we now have specially made "blunt wraps"—anathema to traditionalists— meant to ease the inhalation through lighter paper and fruit flavors.

14

BONG

IN 2013, archaeologists digging in the Caucasus Mountains in Southern Russia made a discovery that proved ancient Scythian cannabis culture was more involved than previously understood. Along with the ornate jewelry of an aristocratic Scythian family, the archaeologists found an ancient water pipe with residue containing both cannabis and opium, a mix the scientists believe was smoked by Scythian kings before leading troops into battle. The multi-piece water pipes are the first known smoking devices to use water as a way to mellow the harshness of smoke. Today, bongs are among the most popular methods of cannabis delivery for that very reason, and can be found in myriad glass varieties, as well as nearly indestructible polymers for the clumsier cannabis user.

THE VOLCANO VAPORIZER

IN THE YEAR 2000, cannabis smoking became obsolete. Sure, people still do it, but for years now, there has been a much safer option that, by all accounts, works far better than the rolling papers you're used to. A futuristic cone befitting the year of its release, the Volcano, first created by Storz & Bickel GmbH & Co., was one of the original devices that could heat cannabis enough to produce inhalable THC and CBD vapor, but not enough to actually combust the flowers and turn them into potentially harmful smoke. Vaporizers are as common as cell phones among some cannabis enthusiasts today, but the Volcano is still going strong even in these days of dabs, g-pens and Paxes.

GREENHAND JOINT

FROM THE SLEEPY TOWN OF Albany, Oregon, a cannabis genius who has yet to see 30 makes his living in perhaps the most interesting niche industry to have grown from the legalization trend. Tony Greenhand is a sculptor, a smoker and a salesman, making perfect replicas of watermelons, architectural works and animals. Each of them are also fully smokeable joints. One client even hired Greenhand to make joint versions of a Glock, a grenade and an AK-47. The latter required a pound and a half of bud.

BUTANE HASH OIL

FOR MILLENNIA, people have been taking cannabis flowers and concentrating them using various techniques. Until recently, the resulting concentrate was known as hash and was rolled into cigarettes or pressed into hookah cakes known as shisha. But as technology has become more and more in touch with the cannabis world, extraction techniques have advanced to the point that hash concentrates are fundamentally different from what we've known as hash for thousands of years. The new version, butane hash oil or BHO—which is almost entirely made up of THC—is created by soaking cannabis in butane, which brings the THC out of the flowers and leaves everything else behind. When the butane is burned off, pure THC resin remains. This is then smoked by placing a bit of it on the end of a needle and attaching it to a bong or pipe with a titanium head, which heats up the oil and allows the user to take a hit. Concentrates are now one of the fastest growing medical and recreational markets in legal states.

LOUIS PASTEUR STATUE

ONE OF THE MOST often-repeated apocryphal cannabis culture legends has to do with the origins of the term 420 to describe the leafy green. The term is ubiquitous among cannabis users and has even turned April 20 into a "high" holiday among enthusiasts, which helps explain why its origin stories are as plentiful as ancient creation myths. But by far the most popular is that five students at California's San Rafael High School in the early 1970s (pictured sitting below smoking a joint before a round of disc golf) began using 4:20 as a code for the grass they'd smoke each afternoon at that time. Their meeting place? A statue of famed scientist Louis Pasteur on the school's campus (pictured opposite).

TRIPLE BEAM BALANCE

"Tap my cell and the phone in the basement
My team supreme, stay clean
Triple beam lyrical dream...."
— *The Notorious B.I.G.*

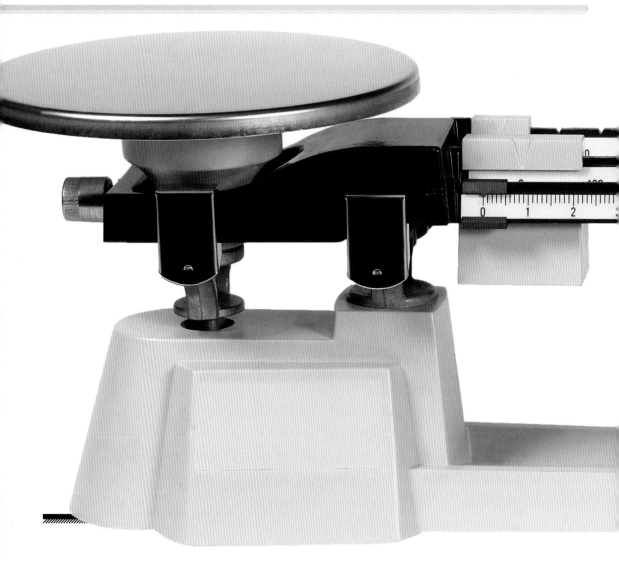

BEFORE IT WAS fodder for one of the world's most famous lyricists and long before it was replaced by the more convenient and portable digital scale, the triple beam balance was the only game in town for measuring your cannabis accurately. Whether it was to sell or just to ration one's stash, weighing with a triple beam made generations of cannabis users just as handy with lab equipment as a high school chemistry teacher. Before each use, the scale had to be calibrated and prepared—and after all that trouble, there was still a .05g margin for error. With the advent of the digital scale the measuring mechanism began to fall out of favor, but "triple beam" is still a cultural touchstone in the cannabis world.

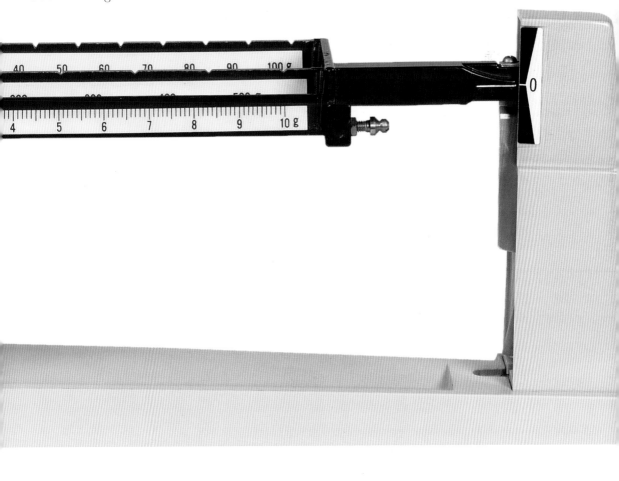

20

MONEY COUNTER

THE MODERN banknote counter traces its roots back to the first digital machine for that purpose created by the Tokyo Calculating Machine Works in the 1960s, but the first automatic money counter was created in the 1920s for use by the tellers at the Federal Reserve Bank. By eliminating the need to count the bills by hand, the workers became more efficient and the counts were more accurate. Before long technologies like counterfeit detection were added to counters to further incorporate them into everyday banking practice. But bankers weren't the only ones to take advantage of the time-saving technology, and soon cash businesses of all stripes started utilizing the money counter. In U.S. states where legal cannabis has been enacted, dispensary owners find counters to be indispensable, as their cash-only businesses can rake in tens of thousands in profit in just a few hours.

PAGER

THE FIRST ONE-WAY paging system was put to use by the Detroit Police in 1928 and relied on A.M. radio. By 1949, that technology, which used vacuum tubes, had found a new home at New York and London hospitals, and pagers almost exclusively remained the accessory of medical professionals for decades. It wasn't until 1986, when Motorola released the eventual bestselling Bravo numeric pager, that the beeper found a home among the underground network of cannabis users who were still a decade away from even the most basic medical use laws. It was now easier than ever to make and keep a connect, and easier to become that connect, with a pager. By 1996, two-way pager messaging—the precursor to today's text message—upped the ante yet again by eliminating the necessity of a home phone to get in touch.

ZIP-TOP BAG

FROM THE PRESERVATION of PB&J lunches to the protection of vinyl records to the easy conveyance of cannabis, Steven Ausnit—a refugee from Stalinist Romania and inventor of the original plastic zipper bag—brought storage convenience into the space age. Ausnit began his experiments with plastic zippers in 1951, four years after his family's escape from Romania. He worked for a decade until he heard of a Japanese company that had found a way to incorporate the zipper into the bag itself. In 1962 he discovered the Japanese model, improved upon it, and before long Ziploc was the gold standard for storing perishables—keeping cannabis stink-free with the simple equation of blue+yellow=green.

VACUUM SEALER

OFTEN HAWKED ON TV as a tool to extend the shelf life of food and avoid freezer burn, inventive weed enthusiasts quickly found a use for the vacuum sealer outside the kitchen. The modern and portable vacuum sealer was first introduced in the mid-'80s, and the handy appliance has since been used on cannabis for a variety of reasons. These include anything from maintaining the stash's freshness to providing convenient storage. But vacuum sealing bud also has a huge bonus: peace of mind. While removing oxygen from the bag, the tight packaging also contains the smell, no matter how strong the chronic. This allows the product to be stored, transferred, sold and carried with discretion. The benefits are simple—it eliminates any obvious signs of bud in the house, glove compartment or gym bag.

CANNABIS OIL

CANNABIS OIL is a mix of a vegetable or nut-based oil and ground marijuana, intended to let cooks add a hint of hashish to their meals. Users who don't want to sully their lungs with smoke can devise cannabis-infused concoctions like quiches, breads, meat marinades and even salad dressings. Many marijuana enthusiasts make their own oils at home, personalizing the oil to their needs—this is especially common since legalization began sweeping the western U.S. Chefs have also picked up on this trend, penning cookbooks and creating menus around the popular plant. When you digest cannabis the plant's effects are less intense but often last longer than smoke. Though the THC compounds move through the system more slowly (creating a less immediately intense response), the high lasts an average of four hours longer, so medical patients can be free from pain and nausea for longer stretches of time.

25

THE VENDING MACHINE

IN FEBRUARY 2015, one of the most common service items to be found in America, the vending machine, was put to a new use that made cannabis patients and legal recreational users across the country rejoice at the new ease with which they could get their green. Seattle had stocked the U.S.'s first vending machine, the exact same model that doles out Snickers and Sour Patch Kids—or leaves them tantalizingly stuck on a precarious perch—in towns all over the world. The machines, known as ZaZZZ, were first placed in dispensaries that required a medical cannabis card to enter. This made sure that only legal cannabis purchasers could make use of the vending machines, but as more states and countries legalize, the pot vending machine could be a staple of the future business.

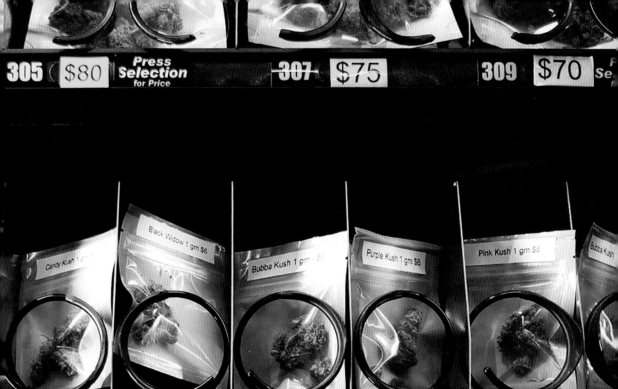

305 $80 **Press Selection** for Price 307 $75 309 $70

Candy Kush 1 gm

Black Widow 1 gm $6

Bubba Kush 1 gm - $6

Purple Kush 1 gm $6

Pink Kush 1 gm $6

Bubba Kush

405 $6 406 $6 407 $6 408 $6 409 $5 **SALE**

Master Kush 1/8 oz $20

Candy Kush 1/8 oz $20

Pink Kush 1/8 oz $20

505 $20 506 $20 507 $20 508 $3 509

HENRY VIII'S LAW

BORN IN 1491, King Henry VIII is best known for his six marriages and his consequent creation of the Church of England. Often ignored in history class, however, is the Tudor King's hemp mandate. In 1533, he ordered all farmers to plant a quarter acre of hemp for every 60 acres of land they owned. In contrast to most of today's growers, they were punished if they didn't grow hemp—facing a fine of 3 shillings and 4 pence for breaking Henry VIII's law. The law was written because the plant was necessary to make riggings, nets, sails, pennants and maps for the British Navy. In light of his religious Reformation, Henry had to ensure his navy was fully suited should the Roman Catholic world rise against him. When the crown eventually fell to his daughter Queen Elizabeth I, she ordered more hemp to be grown, with stiffer penalties for farmers ignoring the law. England was facing war with Spain, and products made with hemp would eventually outfit the Royal Navy ships used to defeat the Spanish Armada in 1588.

BHANG

FROM STREET STALLS and pushcarts all over northern India, locals and tourists alike can be found enjoying the *bhang lassi*, a milkshake made with spices, yogurt or milk, rosewater and bhang—cannabis mixed with water and rolled into balls. For devout Hindus, the drink is an important part of religious festivals like New Year's celebrations, but the *bhang lassi* is also the northern Indian equivalent of an after-work happy hour, with businessmen and laborers settling down with a cannabis shake after a day's toil. Government-sanctioned shops sell the drinks all over the country, continuing a tradition with ancient Hindu roots that has been practiced in India for millennia.

28

DUGOUT

CONSISTING OF a piece of wood with two hollows—one that fits a cigarette-shaped one hitter and the other that can hold a ration of cannabis—and another piece of wood that hinges shut, the dugout offers dual benefits to cannabis users. First, not everyone wants to smoke an entire bowl, blunt or joint: the dugout offers an easy way to smoke just a little. Second the time, space and stamina to smoke a larger portion all at once isn't something everyone possesses. The dugout, which has murky origins but has enjoyed a surge in popularity since Colorado and Washington became the first U.S. states to legalize cannabis, allows both of these types of smokers to tote and toke their green with discretion and ease.

29

CIGARETTE
ONE-HITTER

DERIVED FROM THE CHILLUM, the straight, conical pipe used by Hindu monks for millennia during sacred rites involving cannabis, the one-hitter, also known as the oney, oney hitter, hitter, bat or tay, is part of the essential kit for on-the-go cannabis users all over the world. Providing a single serving of about 25mg of cannabis—or tobacco, as most U.S. states are still forced to sell these as "tobacco tasters"—the one-hitter gives discretion to cannabis users all over the world. The one-hitter is so ubiquitous, in fact, that it's inspired derivations, including those with spring-loaded ash ejectors and serrated teeth for cutting into the packed greenery at the bottom of your dugout.

30

PAX VAPORIZER

WHEN THE FIRST Pax vaporizers hit shelves in 2012, the design, utility and price (upwards of $250 for some models) were all compared to something Apple might make. In a world rapidly normalizing cannabis use, an iPod for weed was exactly what the market wanted, and the Pax seemed to be just that with its charging station, easy-read battery light and super simple use. Since this first explosion of modern design into the cannabis culture, Pax Labs has released the Pax 2 and Pax 3, which vaporize loose leaf like the original, as well as the Pax Era, which is for use with concentrates created exclusively for the Pax—another way the Pax mirrors Apple's famously closed systems.

THE HASHEESH EATER

HASH, THE POTENT form of cannabis made from pressed kief, was a common cure for lockjaw and other nagging, painful diseases throughout the 19th century. In 1857, Fitz-Hugh Ludlow, a graduate of Union College in Schenectady, New York, published his account of eating massive quantities of hashish provided to him by a friend (title page pictured). His background in classical learning, coupled with his vivid descriptions of hallucinations that must have required unbelievable doses of hash to see, became the basis for a bohemian literary connection with cannabis that saw periodic revivals throughout the 20th century, from the beatniks of the 1950s to the hippies of Haight-Ashbury.

THE

HASHEESH EATI

BEING PASSAGES FROM THE

LIFE OF A PYTHAGOREA

" Weave a circle round him thrice,
And close your eyes with holy dread,
For he on honey-dew hath fed,
And drunk the milk of Paradise."
KUBLA KHAN.

NEW YORK:
HARPER & BROTHERS, PUBLISHERS,
FRANKLIN SQUARE.

1857.

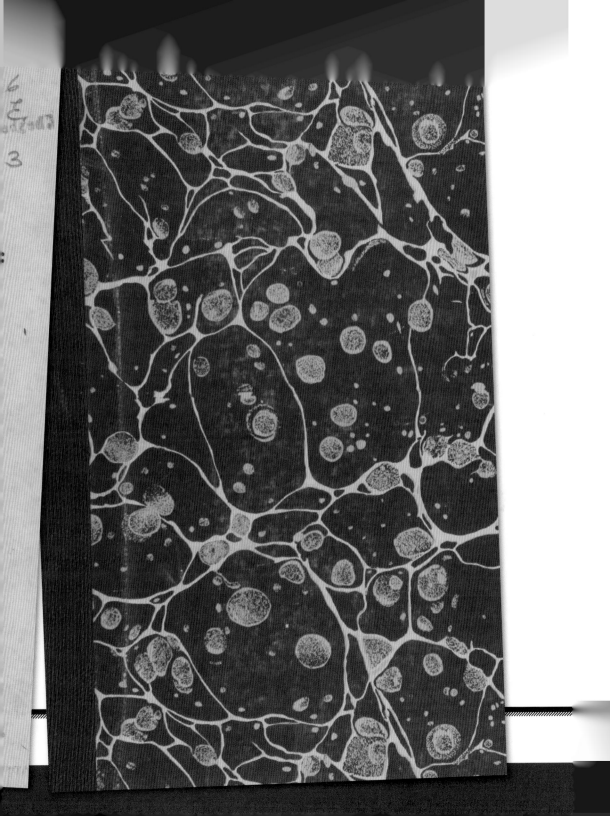

32

HASH BUTTER

THROUGHOUT ITS HISTORY, people have been inventive with their cannabis—smoking it, drinking it as tea, using it as incense or extracting the THC to use for cooking. One of the earliest accounts of extracting THC to cook comes from ancient India, where recipes called for the cannabis to be sautéed in ghee—clarified butter still used in your favorite curry dishes—in order to be effective. Today, THC extraction is crucial to making potent edibles with hash butter (or canna butter). In the most common way of making edibles, the cannabis must be heated slowly in order to change the THC from its acid form to a psychoactive form. This process is called decarboxylation. Once heated with melted, unsalted butter, it makes for the perfect ingredient in those special cookies, or any dish you might use butter in—including anything from Beef Wellington to cherry pie.

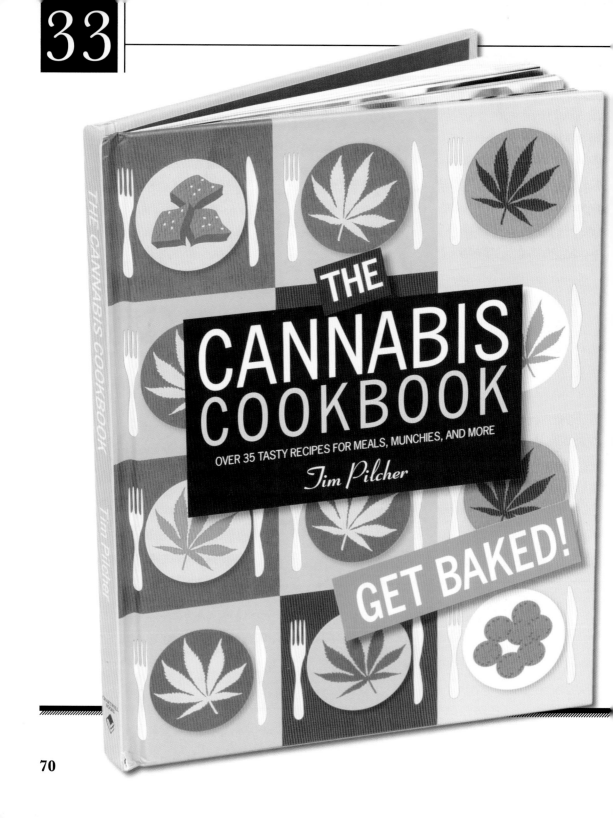

33

THE CANNABIS COOKBOOK

THE CANNABIS COOKBOOK

Tim Pilcher

THE
CANNABIS
COOKBOOK

OVER 35 TASTY RECIPES FOR MEALS, MUNCHIES, AND MORE

Tim Pilcher

GET BAKED!

CANNABIS COOKBOOK

WHEN THE first American cookbook appeared on shelves in 1796, the recipe collection was already an established genre of saleable printed words dating, according to some historians, from the 600s B.C. in Sicily. Amelia Simmons, who wrote *American Cookery*, held true to a principle that has since come full circle—locally sourcing sustainable ingredients. Simmons used ingredients like pumpkin, squash and turkey that were available all over the American frontier. When cannabis became legal in Colorado and Washington in 2012, a resurgent local food trend blended with the DIY farming culture of cannabis to produce a new phenomenon: cannabis chefs. Using flavorless cannabis and butters derived from local harvests as their main weapons, these ganja gourmands have made a business of cannabis dinner parties, restaurants and, perhaps most profitably, cookbooks like Jim Pilcher's (pictured). Amelia Simmons might not have been able to handle cannabutter snickerdoodles, but she'd at least appreciate the impetus behind cannabis cookbooks, which seek to share nonsmoke-based options for cannabis patients and enthusiasts everywhere.

34

THE BROWNIE

THOUGH CANNABIS EDIBLES have been around for centuries, from cannabis teas in ancient China to Moroccan hashish jams and preserves, the modern pot brownie was popularized by Alice B. Toklas, life partner of writer Gertrude Stein and author of *The Alice B. Toklas Cookbook*, in which appears the recipe for "Haschich Fudge" [sic]. Since Toklas's recipe, published in 1954, the pot brownie has been the go-to delivery method for first-timers leery of smoking, users wishing to eliminate the telltale odor from their cannabis experience and those who want to fuse their love for cannabis with their chocoholism.

35

MASON JAR

WHEN FIVE BROTHERS named Ball borrowed $200 from their uncle to start a home canning company and began making glass containers in 1886, they couldn't have known that their jars would become ubiquitous for everything from fancy cocktails to salads to the stench-free and preservative storage of green buds or decarbed canna butter. Though the Ball mason jar is still the gold standard for design-minded or DIY-inspired cannabis users, Ball has also grown into one of the largest makers of beverage cans in the world.

MANGO

TERPENES—the compounds that give some flowers, like cannabis, and some fruits, like mangoes, their distinct scent and flavor profiles—can pair together like food with fine wine. While some cannabis enthusiasts and foodies use this fact to create 12-course cannabis flights paired with plates to complement each strain's terpenes, others are just as satisfied with one of the oldest cannabis pairings in the world: mangoes. Cultivation of the sweet stone fruit goes back 6,000 years to the Indian subcontinent, where priests would also begin to understand the psychoactive properties of cannabis. Just as ginger clears the palate before bites of a sushi dinner, eating mango before a toke can both make the bud taste better and make your high more pronounced as the terpenes of the two plants blend.

DIXIE ELIXIRS

WHEN CANNABIS was legalized in Colorado and Washington, one of the first markets to show a noticeable uptick was cannabis edibles. This is unsurprising: Many people who may have wanted to try cannabis had been turned off by the necessity of smoking, and eating a piece of candy is much easier than rolling a blunt or maintaining a bong. But one upstart idea surprised many first-time cannabis customers and might have made more sense to the happy hour sensibilities of the young professional crowd newly legal cannabis hoped to attract: imbibable cannabis. Enter Dixie Elixirs, which offers soft drinks infused with THC. Meticulously measured and with serving sizes clearly labeled, getting one's medical or recreational cannabis had never been as easy as popping a bottle before. With more and more commentators of the opinion that cannabis is safer than alcohol, companies like Dixie Elixirs are helping to put cannabis in a socially acceptable and easily digestible position.

38

ARIZONA "BIG CAN"

ANYONE WHO has ever walked past their corner store, delicatessen or bodega and seen a curious sticker on the door reading "I Love Big Cans" may have wondered one of several things: Why are these 23-ounce behemoths still only 99 cents? Who needs this much iced tea? To whom, exactly, is this sticker funny? As with many things in life, a puff of some good green will enlighten you as to at least two of these questions.

The story of pot culture's relationship with Arizona's big cans begins with the Great Blunt Schism. For blunt smokers, there are two camps: those who use the outer leaf when they roll and those who don't. For those who do, the limp outer leaf needs to be kept damp in order to bind the blunt together.

Enter the delicious, sweaty Arizona can right out of the gas station ice box. Arizona began manufacturing canned iced tea in 1992, but its big can branding hit an apex in 2008 when they teamed up with golf legend Arnold Palmer to produce his eponymous iced tea-lemonade beverage. While the blunt roller crafts his or her inner leaf, the outer leaf is stuck placidly to the outside of the can. And after that blunt is rolled and smoked, it will be abundantly clear that it's you who needs that much tea, and that simple grade school humor is often all it takes to induce a laughing fit. The best part is, all of this convenience didn't even cost a whole buck.

39

FLAVORED ROLLING PAPERS

THE EARLIEST known rolling papers were probably brought to France, where the Lacroix family were the first to mass manufacture them, by French soldiers. Their biggest client, Napoleon, contracted them to make cigarette papers for his soldiers, who each received a ration of tobacco. In 1865, the company changed their name to "RizLa+" when the paper formula switched to include rice. Lacroix continued their innovation as they created the cigarette rolling machine and later, in 1906, they introduced the first flavored papers. While the original flavors from RizLa+ were simply menthol and strawberry, modern rolling paper companies like Juicy Jays have expanded the flavor list to include everything from milk chocolate to Jamaican Rum.

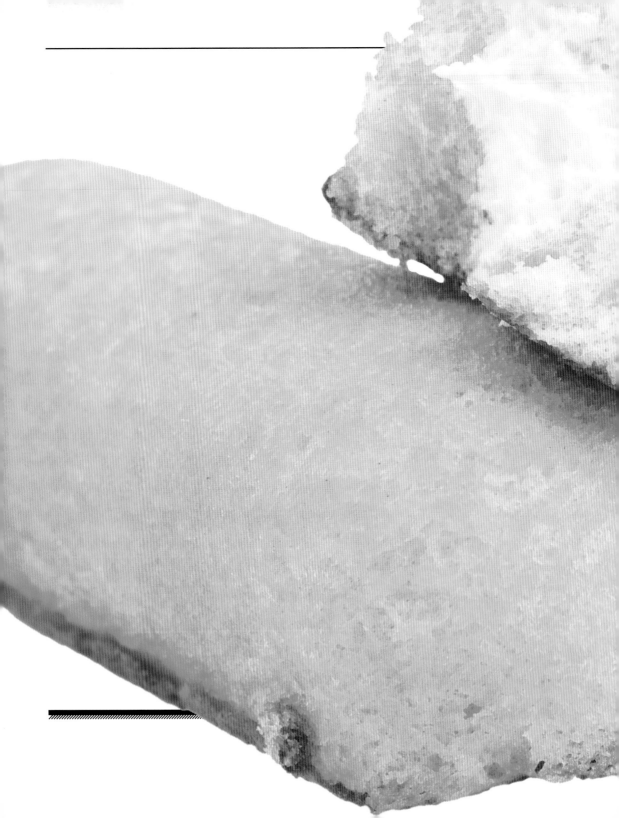

40

TWINKIE

WHEN JAMES ALEXANDER DEWAR,
a baker with the Continental Baking
Company, created the first Twinkie in 1930,
he couldn't have known that he'd created
the quintessential American snack food for
the 20th century. Apple pie might have a
monopoly on the "all-American foodstuff"
market, but the Twinkie isn't far behind.
Whether it was an American GI enjoying a
care package from Hostess, a 1950s schoolkid
opening up his or her brown paper bag or
a ravenous toker on the hunt for something
to hit that elusive spot—Americans have
gone crazy for the simple cake and cream
concoctions for decades, both in the original
banana cream flavor and the more well-known
vanilla. In an age generally associated with the
Leave it to Beaver school of cultural norms, the
Twinkie was the one snack that bridged the
monstrous gap between buttoned-up 1950s
folks and their counter-cultural counterparts.

41

HALF BAKED ICE CREAM

WHEN TWO self-admitted hippies took a $5 correspondence course in ice cream making from Penn State, they were making the first investment in what would soon become an ice cream empire. In 1978, Jerry Greenfield and Ben Cohen opened their first ice cream shop. Ben & Jerry's is now a global phenomenon known just as much for their inventive flavor names as their no-holds-barred approach to creating those flavors. Some of their most successful inspirations have also become mainstays of munchie culture, from Cherry Garcia (named for one of cannabis culture's greatest figureheads) to the ever-beloved Chunky Monkey. But the Ben & Jerry's product most directly associated with the munchies is, by far, Half Baked. The concoction of vanilla and chocolate ice cream with baked fudge brownies and chocolate chip cookie dough is, as *Complex* magazine put it, "The only thing you should be consuming when you're completely baked."

SHAKESPEARE'S "SONNET 76"

Why is my verse so barren of new pride?
So far from variation or quick change?
Why with the time do I not glance aside
To new-found methods and to compounds strange?
Why write I still all one, ever the same,
And keep invention in a noted weed,
That every word doth almost tell my name,
Showing their birth and where they did proceed?
—from Sonnet 76, William Shakespeare

THERE HAVE BEEN many creative thinkers in the centuries following Shakespeare's day who are suspected to have "kept invention in a noted weed," but close reading of Sonnet 76 in the late 20th century led some to wonder if the Bard himself had drawn inspiration from some "compounds strange" that included cannabis. In 2001, South African researcher Francis Thackeray took it upon himself to analyze the contents of pipes found at Stratford-upon-Avon, Shakespeare's home hamlet. While no definitive proof of cannabis use by the Bard was found, mass to charge ratios that indicated cannabis-based compounds may have been present. Hard evidence of nicotine was found, however.

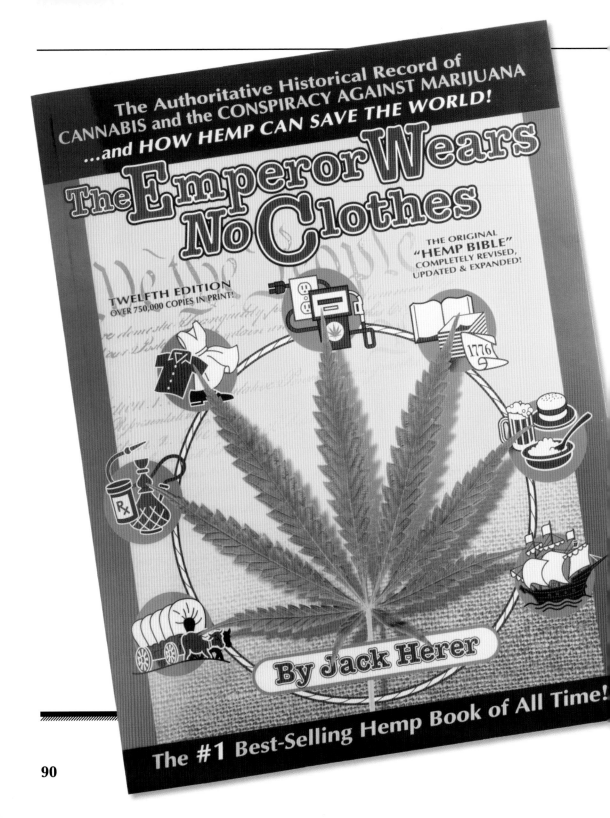

The Authoritative Historical Record of CANNABIS and the CONSPIRACY AGAINST MARIJUANA ...and HOW HEMP CAN SAVE THE WORLD!

The Emperor Wears No Clothes

THE ORIGINAL "HEMP BIBLE" COMPLETELY REVISED, UPDATED & EXPANDED!

TWELFTH EDITION
OVER 750,000 COPIES IN PRINT!

1776

By Jack Herer

The #1 Best-Selling Hemp Book of All Time!

THE EMPEROR WEARS NO CLOTHES

JACK "THE HEMPEROR" HERER is known as one of the most prominent figures in late 20th century cannabis legalization and awareness. He devoted his life to being a cannabis activist—researching and campaigning for decriminalization for nearly 40 years. The crown jewel of his work was his book *The Emperor Wears No Clothes*, published in 1985 (appropriately on hemp paper). Herer spent 12 years compiling the book, which contains historical information about the uses for hemp and the benefits of cannabis. It also details the government's plot to criminalize and suppress the use of the plant instead of using it as a renewable source of food, medicine and fossil fuels. So confident was Herer in *The Emperor Wears No Clothes*, he offered an as-yet unclaimed $100,000 to anyone that could disprove any claims in his "Hemp Bible." To this day, Herer's book has sold more than 700,000 copies and is still cited in conversations of cannabis legalization. When the author died in 2010, his book was made available for free on *jackherer.com*.

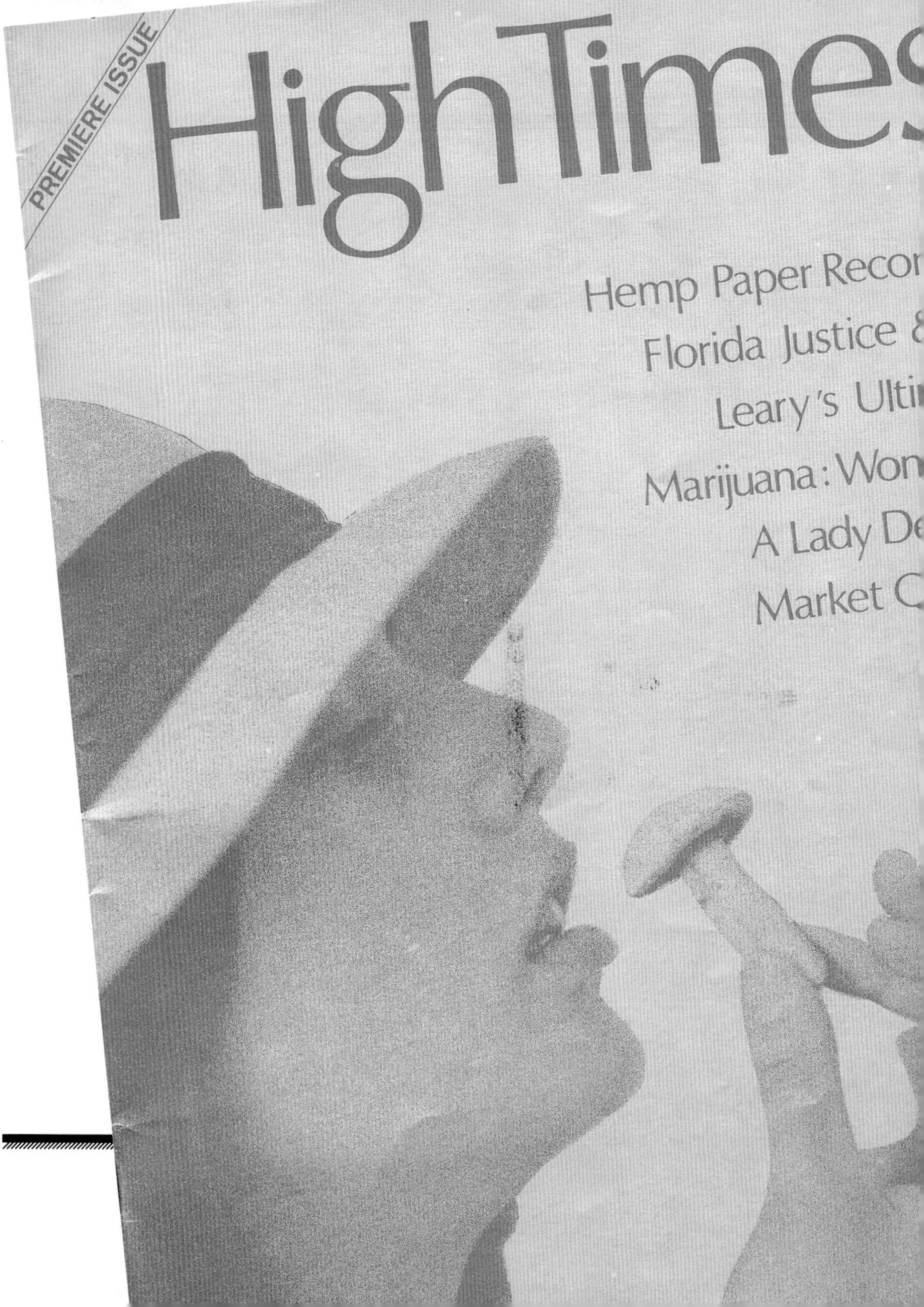

HighTimes

Hemp Paper Recor
Florida Justice &
Leary's Ulti
Marijuana: Won
A Lady De
Market C

FIRST ISSUE OF *HIGH TIMES*

WHILE IT MAY be difficult to fathom in today's hyperconnected world, people partaking in cannabis before the advent of the internet had to rely on friends and family who were "cool" to learn best practices about getting high. Geography may not have posed too onerous a challenge to residents of New York, Los Angeles or any of America's other more pot-friendly enclaves, but those living in the countless small towns and rural areas of the country were out of luck. Fortunately for everyone, the summer of 1974 saw the first issue of *High Times* hit newsstands, and cannabis lovers finally had access to a treasure trove of information about their favorite plant. Founded by journalist, activist and marijuana smuggler Tom Forçade, the magazine has (barring a few interruptions) provided an entertaining mix of instructional information and writing by authors such as Hunter S. Thompson and William S. Burroughs. As marijuana has edged its way into becoming a legitimate market, the magazine has expanded its coverage to provide entrepreneurs and investors looking to cash in on the Green Rush with business tips and advice. It's just one way *High Times* continues to serve the cannabis community, no matter how straight-laced it may become.

The full leaf as well as the buds and trichomes of a Fire Creek plant show the variety of shades to be found in today's meticulously bred cannabis, based on strains collected and catalogued in the 1970s and '80s.

45

PROTEST SIGNS

THE LATE 1960s were marked by free-thinking college students who were actively anti-establishment. Inspired by large-scale protest action taken all over the world, they began sharing ideas in apartments and coffee houses from the Haight to Greenwich Village, and when they did, their plans were typicall hatched over ashtrays smoldering with joints. Fueled by the growing normalization of the counterculture—and its representative plant, cannabis—young adults held tenets of love and peace above all. With cannabis as the linking element, feminists, beatniks, civil rights thinkers and the best minds of a generation took on specters from racism to war.

These movements came to a head in 1968. Just months into the new year, three black students were killed in South Carolina; the Tet Offensive and My Lai Massacre occurred in Vietnam; and Martin Luther King Jr. was assassinated. In April 1968, frustrated students at Columbia University left their incense-and-reefer scented dorms and took to the streets to protest the school's involvement with weapons research for the war in Vietnam.

The NYPD were called six days later and after a violent standoff, 700 people were arrested for crimes from resisting arrest to vandalism—but more than a few were booked for simple pot possession, and in fact the ongoing drug war became a frequent pretense for quashing leftists. The Columbia protests were soon echoed by Sorbonne University students in France just a few weeks later. While they first protested the Paris University at Nanterre shutting down, the violent reaction from the government led more than one million students and workers to march through Paris on May 10. These protests marked the beginning of modern dissent, and cannabis was a huge part of the culture that made the so-called 68-ers famous.

INFLATABLE PROTEST JOINT

LIGHTING UP A JOINT is a staple at any pot legalization rally, protest or 420 march. But nothing gets the protest-attendees or holiday celebrators more attention than the giant inflatable joint that is often in tow. The first pot-protest was held on August 16, 1964, where just one person—Lowell Eggemeier—smoked a joint in front of police officers at the San Francisco Hall of Justice. More than 50 years later, the protests and "smoke-ins" for cannabis reform aren't as subtle as Eggemeier's one man show. In April 2016, 200 cannabis activists upped their joint game and created a 51-foot inflatable joint to march outside of the White House. The same protestors built a second joint of the same size for other "Jaywalks," with giant, balloon-like spliffs making stops in New York and Philadelphia, where the pictured joint could be found outside the 2016 Democratic National Convention. The inflatable joints are a reminder that full legalization has a long road ahead, while celebrating the strides that have already been made.

HUNTER S. THOMPSON MEMORIAL

THE GONZO MOVEMENT wasn't about cannabis in particular, and Hunter S. Thompson was famously loathe to limit his illicit intake to greenery. But the writer who gave us *Fear and Loathing in Las Vegas*, *Hell's Angels* and some of the most innovative political reporting in history was a vocal enthusiast and supporter of legalization. According to a notorious passage in E. Jean Carroll's biography *Hunter: The Strange and Savage Life of Hunter S. Thompson*, each evening Thompson would indulge in "grass" to "take the edge off." After he committed suicide in 2005, friends and colleagues gathered near Thompson's Colorado home to indulge while they fulfilled the writer's final earthly wish—having his ashes shot out of a cannon. In 2017, Thompson's widow plans to release clones of the strains he grew for himself, pleasing his following yet again.

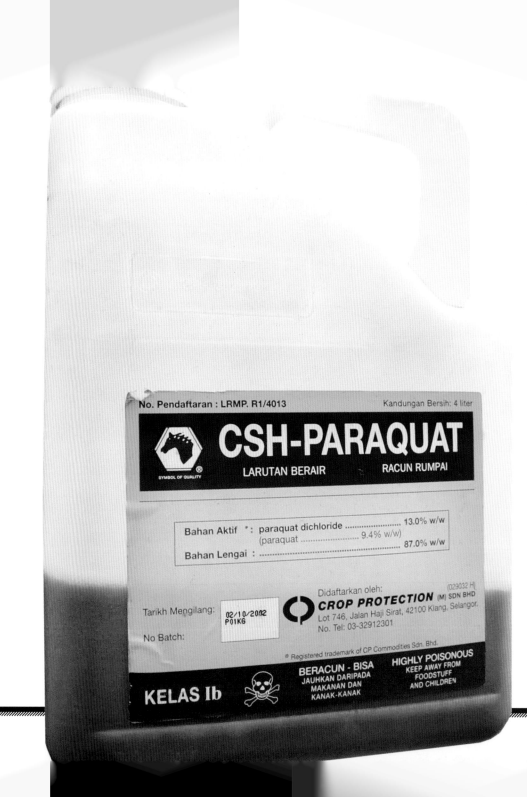

No. Pendaftaran : LRMP. R1/4013   Kandungan Bersih: 4 liter

CSH-PARAQUAT

LARUTAN BERAIR   RACUN RUMPAI

SYMBOL OF QUALITY

Bahan Aktif * : paraquat dichloride .... 13.0% w/w
              (paraquat .... 9.4% w/w)
Bahan Lengai : .... 87.0% w/w

Tarikh Mengilang :   02/10/2002
                      P01K6

No Batch:

Didaftarkan oleh: (029032 H)
CROP PROTECTION (M) SDN BHD
Lot 746, Jalan Haji Sirat, 42100 Klang, Selangor,
No. Tel: 03-32912301

® Registered trademark of CP Commodities Sdn. Bhd.

KELAS Ib

BERACUN - BISA
JAUHKAN DARIPADA
MAKANAN DAN
KANAK-KANAK

HIGHLY POISONOUS
KEEP AWAY FROM
FOODSTUFF
AND CHILDREN

PARAQUAT

THE HISTORY OF North American governments and the controversial, deadly pesticide paraquat begins in 1973, when the Mexican government announced plans to eradicate the country's illegal cannabis crop with it. The move immediately caused concern across the U.S. border that shipments of cannabis north might be tainted with the chemical, which can cause total organ shutdown. By the 1980s, however, the Reagan administration's "Just Say No" Drug Enforcement Administration had no qualms about planning to use paraquat on plants in the U.S., including, according to an *L.A. Times* article of July 28, 1985, on private and tribal land. In fact, one of the Reagan administration's lame-duck maneuvers in 1988 was another attempt (the third since 1983) to allow the widespread use of the deadly pesticide in the U.S. To this day, Paraquat stands as an example of the deadly lengths governments have gone to enforce cannabis prohibition.

49

HASHISH AND MENTAL ILLNESS

WHEN PSYCHIATRY was in its infancy, a 19th-century French thinker named Jacques-Joseph Moreau began to test a hash-related hypothesis: The effects of large doses of hash may help us to better understand those suffering from certain mental disorders. Moreau was a member, along with Alexandre Dumas and Charles Baudelaire, of the famous Club des Hachichins, which met in Paris to consume hash and philosophize. It was his experiences among Parisian society that led him to use cannabis to try proving his notion that mental illness was caused by an imbalance in the brain resulting from the organ being, in Moreau's words, more "irrigated" compared to other organs. His studies were published under the title *Hashish and Mental Illness*. While cannabis in Moreau's mind was primarily a tool for the insight of the analyst, he was nevertheless onto something when he posited that cannabis—currently in use for anxiety, depression, PTSD and other mental disorders—had huge potential for the human psyche.

HASHISH
AND MENTAL ILLNESS

J. J. MOREAU

DEA JACKET

WHEN PRESIDENT NIXON founded the Drug Enforcement Administration with an executive order in July 1973, he officially ended the last vestiges of the open-minded and cannabis-friendly 1960s and began what has now become known as the War on Drugs (which at the time also seemed like a war on the counterculture). The first class of officers was a force of 1,470 special agents with a budget of less than $75 million—currently, the DEA receives $2 billion annually. "Right now," Nixon said, defending his order, "the federal government is fighting the war on drug abuse under a distinct handicap, for its efforts are those of a loosely confederated alliance facing a resourceful, elusive, worldwide enemy." Since the first states legalized medicinal and recreational cannabis, the DEA has come under greater scrutiny—both as abuse of power by law enforcement becomes a more public problem, and as the age-old struggle between federal and state authorities means the DEA has concerned themselves with people not breaking the laws of their state by selling, smoking or owning cannabis.

51

ANGOLA PRISON

ANGOLA, a maximum security prison in Louisiana, is named after the plantation that once stood on the land, which was in turn named for the country from which that plantation's slaves had been taken. Since Angola's gates first opened in 1880, Louisiana has become the most incarcerated state in the union per capita, with one in 86 adult Louisianans in jail as of 2012. Many of those prisoners are serving "three strikes" sentences that mean because of cannabis, they will never be free again. While roughly 725,000 people are arrested each year in the U.S. for cannabis-related crimes, many of these arrests do not end in convictions. The ones that do disproportionately affect the black populations of cities like New Orleans, the major metropolitan area which is served by Angola prison. According to a 2013 study by the ACLU, the disparity between white and black Americans being convicted for cannabis was exponentially larger throughout the entire country.

52

MILE 419.99

THOSE LOOKING TO take home a souvenir from their cannabis pilgrimage to Colorado no longer have the "MILE 420" sign to steal as their trophy. Colorado's Interstate 70 is 450 miles long from east to west, with signs along the way to mark the miles. The Mile 420 marker, about 145 miles east of Denver, was stolen by weed-enthusiasts so frequently that the Colorado Department of Transportation had no choice but to replace it with one that reads "MILE 419.99." While the creative signage succeeded in warding off sticky-fingered stoners at first, Mile 419.99 has once again become a popular destination on an otherwise uninteresting stretch of highway. Some congregate for pictures with the now internet-famous sign, while others go for drives just to see if it's real. The 419.99 marker still goes missing on occasion, but mostly serves as a photo opportunity for stoners who appreciate the state of Colorado's sense of humor—or at least awareness.

STERILE

INTERIOR IF SEAL IS NOT BROKEN

INTERIOR SI EL SELLO NO ESTÁ ROTO

INTÉRIEUR SI LE SCELLÉ N'EST PAS CASSÉ

Name
Nom
Nombre:

Room
Chambre
Habitación:

Time
Heure
Hora:

Date
Date
Fecha:

Made in • Fabriqué au • Fabricado en USA

URINE TEST

IN JUNE OF 1995 the U.S. Supreme Court ruled that a Vernonia, Washington, School District law requiring drug tests for all high school athletes, whether reasonable suspicion existed or not, was constitutional. This was the beginning of the modern era of urinalysis used not as a medical diagnostic for kidney function, UTIs and other conditions, but as a test for athletes, job applicants and workers to pass. Before this court decision, drug testing had been regularly struck down by lower courts on the basis of our protection against illegal search and seizure enshrined in the Bill of Rights, but corporations began to make it normal practice in the 1980s, when anti-drug fervor was at its highest and "Just Say No" was one of Ronald (and Nancy) Reagan's pet slogans.

"YOUR BRAIN ON DRUGS"

"THIS IS YOUR BRAIN." A pristine shelled egg is held in front of the camera. "This is your brain on drugs." The egg is cracked into a frying pan. This illustration of being "fried" or "burning out" was the most enduring symbol of the "Just Say No" era for a generation of American youths—not that it stopped cannabis use in the U.S. The Partnership for a Drug-Free America, the group responsible for the 1987 commercial, currently calls itself the Partnership for Drug-Free Kids. The organization strived to teach people how to talk to their kids about drugs, including tough questions like "But you smoked when you were younger, why shouldn't I?"

H.R. 5484

Ninety-ninth Congress of the United States of America

AT THE SECOND SESSION

Begun and held at the City of Washington on Tuesday, the twenty-first day of January, one thousand nine hundred and eighty-six

An Act

To strengthen Federal efforts to encourage foreign coopera-
tion in eradicating illicit drug crops and in halting
international drug traffic, to improve enforcement of
Federal drug laws and enhance interdiction of illicit
drug shipments, to provide strong Federal leadership in
establishing effective drug abuse prevention and education programs, to expand Federal support for drug abuse
treatment and rehabilitation efforts, and for other
purposes.

Be it enacted by the Senate and House of Representatives
of the United States of America in Congress assembled,

1 SECTION 1. SHORT TITLE.

2   This Act may be cited as the ``Anti-Drug Abuse Act of

3 1986''.

4 SEC. 2. ORGANIZATION OF ACT.

5   This Act is organized as follows:

TITLE I--ANTI-DRUG ENFORCEMENT

Subtitle A--Narcotics Penalties and Enforcement Act of 1986
Subtitle B--Drug Possession Penalty Act of 1986
Subtitle C--Juvenile Drug Trafficking Act of 1986
Subtitle D--Assets Forfeiture Amendments Act of 1986
Subtitle E--Controlled Substance Analogue Enforcement Act of 1986
Subtitle F--Continuing Drug Enterprise Act of 1986
Subtitle G--Controlled Substances Import and Export Act Penalties
Enhancement Act of 1986
Subtitle H--Money Laundering Control Act of 1986
Subtitle I--Armed Career Criminals
Subtitle J--Authorization of Appropriations for Drug Law
Enforcement
Subtitle K--State and Local Narcotics Control Assistance
Subtitle L--Study on the Use of Existing Federal Buildings as
Prisons
Subtitle M--Narcotics Traffickers Deportation Act
Subtitle N--Freedom of Information Act
Subtitle O--Prohibition on the Interstate Sale and Transportation
of Drug Paraphernalia
Subtitle P--Manufacturing Operations
Subtitle Q--Controlled Substances Technical Amendments
Subtitle R--Precursor and essential chemical review
Subtitle S--White House Conference for A Drug Free America
Subtitle T--Common carrier operation under the influence of

55

ANTI-DRUG ABUSE ACT

BY THE MID-1980s, the War on Drugs had ballooned to its most bloated state: The advent of freebase cocaine meant that drug use was more prevalent than ever in the U.S. Because cannabis shares Schedule I status with cocaine and heroin, users saw the crackdown affect green bud just as often as crack rock. The Anti-Drug Abuse Act strengthened federal power in a number of ways, from allowing economic penalties against countries who did not go along with the U.S.'s drug policy to re-establishing the concept of "mandatory minimums" for drug sentences. According to a 2014 study by the ACLU called "Racial Disparities in Sentencing," mandatory minimums imposed dramatically harsher penalties on crack than powder cocaine or cannabis, centering longer prison sentences in crack-devastated urban centers.

56

MAUREEN DOWD'S 6/4/2014 *NEW YORK TIMES* OP-ED

WHEN PROLIFIC *New York Times* columnist Maureen Dowd was tasked with going to the newly legal state of Colorado and sampling its wares, she couldn't have known she would become the poster child for irresponsible consumption and a thorn in the sides of cannabis activists who took issue with her column, rather patronizingly titled "Don't Harsh Our Mellow, Dude." Upon arrival in Colorado, Dowd proceeded to purchase a cannabis chocolate bar, the serving size for which was a single pip, and ate most of the bar in one sitting. "I became convinced that I had died and no one was telling me," she wrote in the op-ed, which seemed to suggest that her less-than-ideal experience was the fault of cannabis rather than poor direction-reading. As a result, the cannabis community mobilized for the first time as a legal entity.

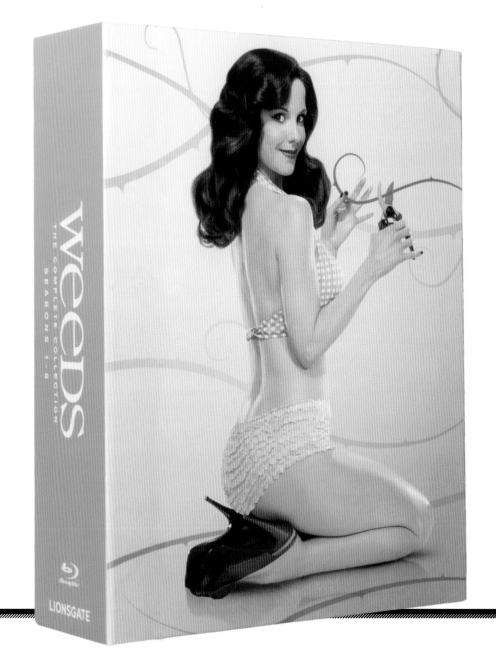

WEEDS: THE COMPLETE SERIES

IF THERE WERE ever any confusion as to what the main subject matter of Showtime's *Weeds* is, their distinctive green-leafed DVD covers give it away. Running eight seasons from 2005–2012, the Jenji Kohan-created comedy follows Nancy Botwin (Mary-Louise Parker), who starts selling cannabis to support her family after her husband dies. While conversations or depictions of pot in pop culture were often limited to stereotypical burnouts and troublemakers, suburban mom Nancy helped evolve the conversation and revealed to audiences that pot smokers are everywhere—no matter the neighborhood.

The high-profile show quickly garnered critical acclaim for its unconventional themes. As with many controversial topics, television often plays a role in changing and modernizing public perceptions. When *Weeds* premiered in 2005, few mainstream Americans were aware of the lengths pot had traveled since the 1960s, and it was Nancy Botwin and her circle of endearingly dysfunctional characters that introduced them to the wonders of the dispensary, tinctures, candies and tunnels used to smuggle the drug (as well as illegal immigrants) from Mexico. It also showed a side of cannabis—as a cash crop and a medicine—that few had yet seen in the real world.

58

STASH BOX

IT COULD BE anything from a simple Tupperware container to the box that once held your prized Air Jordan XIIs, but a stash box is a must-have for cannabis users who lack the luxury of leaving their leaf out on the coffee table for all to see. A shoebox falls on the decidedly lo-fi end of the stash box spectrum, with cigar boxes or—no judgment—wine crates being the universal standard and small safes designed to look like books or cans of Coke bringing up the more paranoia-friendly end. But the most elegant solution to the problem of how and where to stash might be the Japanese puzzle box. While scholars disagree about the exact origins of the puzzle box, Japanese craftsmen, whose traditional methods of temple-making used neither nails nor glue, have been crafting the trinkets for export since the early 20th century. The boxes will remain closed until the correct sequence of moves has been made, and some require as many as 50 perfectly executed entries.

59

HERB GRINDER

THE MODERN cannabis grinder—used to turn raw flowers into smokeable, vapable or bakeable form—is a sophisticated machine compared to the first industrial grinders, introduced by Lewis Heim, an engineer who worked for The Ball and Bearing Roller Company in 1905. Meant for apothecaries and pharmacists, the "centerless" grinder, as it was known, made processing plant matter into medicine a much easier proposition than a mortar and pestle. Over time, cannabis-specific grinders were devised, the most common of which to modern smokers is the four-piece grinder. This device features a two-part grinding mechanism consisting of a cap and base with alternating grooves for breaking up flowers, a receptacle for the ground material and a kief-catcher, which collects the extra-fine crystals that slip through the mesh of the first receptacle.

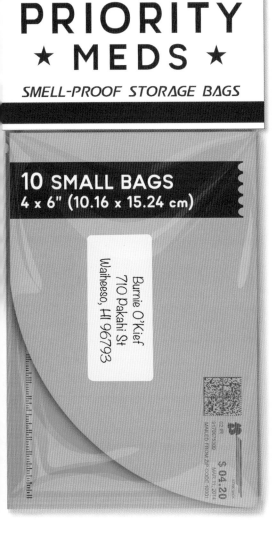

60

SMELL-PROOF BAGS

HOW CAN ONE best explain the panic of stashing a plain-old Ziploc bag full of reefer in your pocket or down your sock and then getting on the subway, only to catch a whiff of the telltale smell moments later? The inner monologue writes itself. "Is it mine? Is it that guy's? Do other people smell it? That girl's looking at me. OK. OK. OK. Be cool." Luckily explanations are no longer necessary, thanks to smell-proof baggies. Stink Sack, for example, began making smell-proof (and later, child-resistant) baggies specifically for cannabis in 2009. They're currently one of about a dozen companies selling similar smell-proof baggies everywhere from Amazon to REI.

61

DRYER SHEET

THE FIRST AMERICAN patent for fabric softener was filed in 1976, but it would be a later innovation—infusing the sweet-smelling liquid into dryer sheets—that made the laundry room staple a stash box must-have. Few items can mask the potent odor of cannabis entirely, but the humble dryer sheet can work wonders for discreet potheads in the same way they help out gym rats forced to carry their bags to the office. One drawback known to anyone who's stored their bud in dryer sheets is how their flowery flavor will stick to anything, including their bowls. So don't be alarmed when your next toke is a bit more Downy fresh than usual.

"MR. X" 'S TESTIMONY

"I do not consider myself a religious person in the usual sense, but there is a religious aspect to some highs. The heightened sensitivity in all areas gives me a feeling of communion with my surroundings, both animate and inanimate."
—*Carl Sagan*

WHEN *MARIHUANA RECONSIDERED* published an eloquent defense of cannabis by a writer using the pseudonym "Mr. X" in 1969, few who read the obscure essay could have guessed that the author would later endear himself to millions of TV viewers as the host of *Cosmos*, the first program to tackle cosmic questions in scientific terms able to be understood by average Americans: Carl Sagan. The essay describes how Sagan began using cannabis 10 years prior to its publication and how it helped him develop an appreciation for the world beyond scientific study, especially the fine arts, for which he claimed to have had no taste before. "The understanding of the intent of the artist which I can achieve when high sometimes carries over to when I'm down," "Mr. X" wrote. "This is one of many human frontiers which cannabis has helped me traverse."

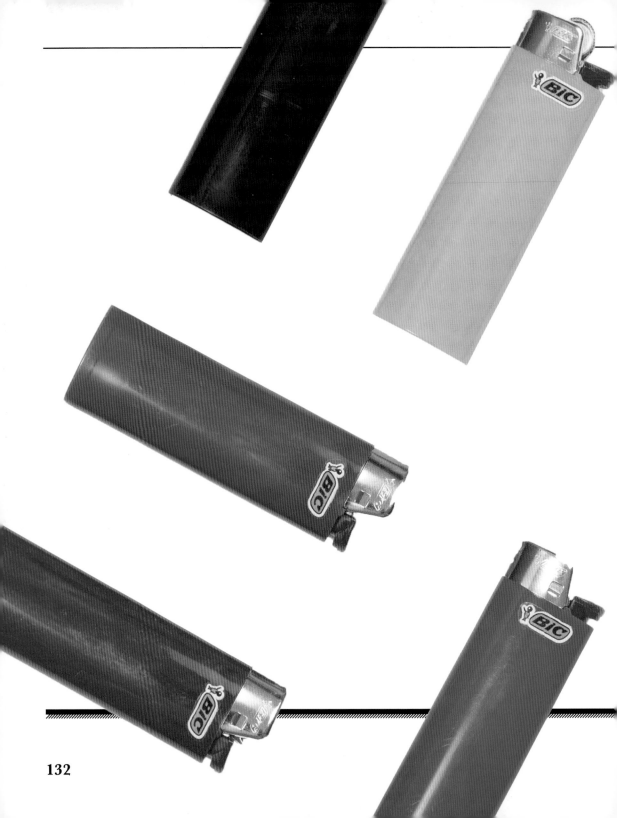

THE BIC
LIGHTER

IN 1973, the French company Sociéte BIC S.A., more commonly known as BIC, expanded their business—known mostly for ballpoint pens—by acquiring a disposable lighter company. That year, they introduced the very first Bic lighter, an item that's now ubiquitous and so easy to use that the Museum of Modern Art has one in its design collection.

The new lighter's safety mechanism freed cannabis users from having to close a Zippo—or worry about burning their fingers—to light more involved apparatus like bongs and bowls. It's not just cannabis users who count the BIC as one of their most important everyday items. From campers to cooks, the BIC is the easiest and most reliable way there is to make fire.

LIGHTERBRO

UNFORTUNATE NAME ASIDE—seriously, was Lighter Bud taken?—the LighterBro is the most important innovation to affect the lighter since the Bic first appeared on shelves. A metal sleeve the exact size of a standard Bic lighter, the LighterBro is a stoner-specific Swiss Army-type knife including a small screwdriver that doubles as a poker, scissors for cutting open those pesky vacuum bags and a bottle opener to help combat dry mouth. Since the LighterBro filed for a patent in 2010, it has been released in various colors with specific tools and retails on *Amazon.com*.

65

ROACH CLIP

SIMPLE CIGARETTE PAPER has long been one of the most common apparatus for cannabis smoking, and toking from a joint is as time-honored a tradition as any in the world of green bud. Joints are easy to share, get everyone high and are simple to make. There's really only one consistent problem with smoking joints: the last third. Once the joint gets small enough for flame and finger to be close together, lips and hands are in danger of a quick scorching. Enter the humble roach clip. It could be a paper clip, manipulated bobby or safety pin or (preferably) a crocodile clip, which has vaguely joint-sized grooves and provides a safe place to put your fingertips when the joint gets hot.

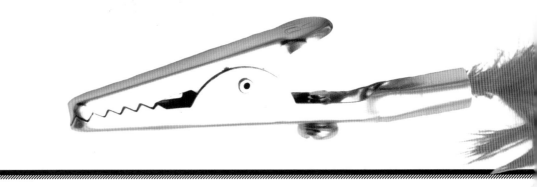

66

HUMIDOR

HUMIDORS ARE ANY containers designed to store tobacco, cigars or cigarettes at an ideal level of humidity. In order to maintain freshness and flavor, they're typically small boxes built from Spanish cedar, which retains moisture better than most woods. The humidity levels are measured through a device called the hygrometer, which was first built by Leonardo da Vinci sometime in the 1480s. While modern hygrometers are digital (and more practical), da Vinci used a balanced scale to measure how much moisture a ball of wool conserved in different temperatures.

Before the 18th century, humidors were simply large tobacco curing barns common in Central America. The first to transform these barns into portable boxes was, according to tradition, Terence Manning—who, upon returning from South Africa to his home in Ireland in 1887, brought back rare woods and techniques in order to craft the first cabinet humidor. Humidors have since become smaller with more refined moisture control, and it's no surprise that people eventually started stashing their stash in one of these functional yet aesthetically pleasing boxes. Recently, companies like Cannador have created humidors specifically made for weed—making small but impactful changes to better benefit bud. These include using mahogany in order to reduce odors left from the traditional Spanish cedar and an advanced humidification system, as cannabis is more likely than tobacco to develop mold.

HACKY SACK

DEBUTING IN 1972, the hacky sack likely missed its largest sales opportunity by three years, passing up the chance to provide every hippie at Woodstock with one of the exercise fads turned quintessential stoner accessories. The little bean bag was created by two Oregon natives, John Stalberger Jr. and Mike Marshall, who set out to create a challenging and fun new way to exercise. By the 1980s, they were ready to sell their invention to Wham-O for $1.5 million. The hacky sack requires a level of coordination that might seem surprising considering the circular field of play is often wreathed in fragrant smoke, but even more than the drum circle, the hacky sack circle is the ultimate gathering for the fleet of foot and cannabis-minded.

ALUMINUM FOIL

TIN WAS first replaced by aluminum in foil making around 1926—aluminum itself was introduced in ingot form in 1888—but it would be decades before aluminum foil, popularized by the Reynolds company, would become a household mainstay, keeping food fresh and controlling the temperature of leftovers all over America. These same freshness-saving qualities—as well as the fact that a tight wrapping of aluminum foil masks numerous smells, from old cheese to new weed—meant that before long, tin foil often played into the cannabis storage scheme for pantry-raiding smokers everywhere. If you're an arts and crafts-type smoker, you can even fashion a rudimentary pipe with it in a pinch.

69

CHILD-PROOF PILL BOTTLE

DR. HENRI J. BREAULT of Tecumseh, Ontario, revolutionized the pharmaceutical industry in 1967 when he invented the modern child-proof pill bottle, requiring both pushing and twisting to open while creating a remarkably good seal. Almost immediately, the familiar translucent orange, white-capped bottles appealed to space saving, design-obsessed and, as always, under the radar cannabis enthusiasts. They make perfect impromptu dugouts for pre-ground bud, and—as dispensaries found out as soon as legalization became the law of the land in some states— pill bottles are also the perfect size for distributing eighth-ounces of legal flower.

70

SPLOOF

THE MERITS OF the dryer sheet for the enterprising cannabis enthusiast are well-documented. Adding a paper towel roll and a rubber band completely changes the game. Just ask generations of secret summer camp, attic and school bathroom tokers. No one knows exactly which weed MacGyver first came up with the idea, or when, but the cannabis world owes them a debt. By placing a dryer sheet around one end of the cardboard roll and securing it with a rubber band, that cloud of reefer smoke you were about to blow out so that everyone could see and smell it is now a formless, sweet-smelling breeze. At least that's the idea. Still—if you're smoking your buds covertly you're doing so at your own risk.

NAPOLEON'S EDICT

THE HISTORY OF cannabis prohibition in the Western world is a long one, often interspersed with tangents into race and class relations, economics and military history. It is this last branch that gave Europe its first prohibition law in 1798 when Napoleon Bonaparte made it a crime for his French soldiers to smoke the hashish they had developed a taste for while conquering Egypt, a Muslim nation where no alcohol was readily available for French troops who were accustomed to a daily wine ration. In France today, prohibition is still the law of the land, representing a relatively unbroken tradition—though a growing political movement led by the socialist party has recently stepped up advocacy for legalization.

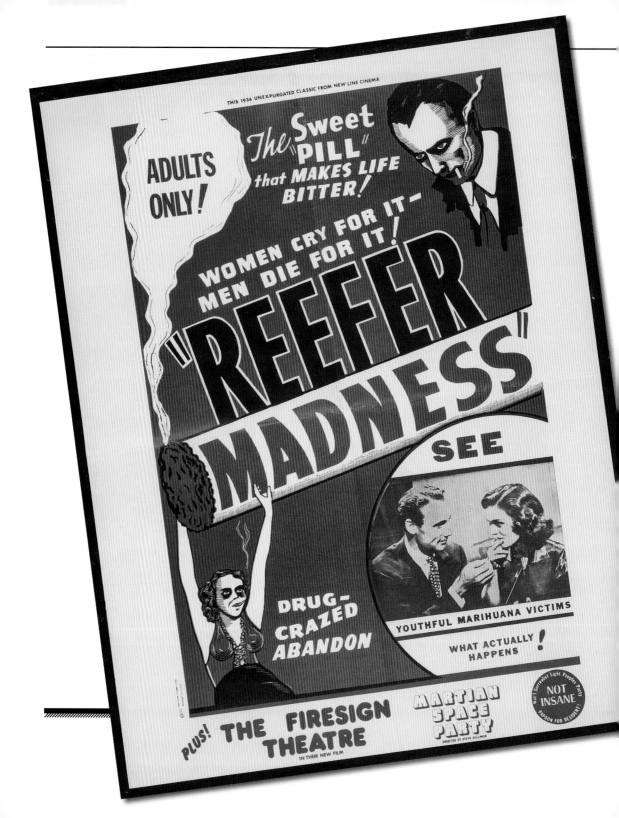

72

REEFER MADNESS POSTER

AFTER INNOCENT HIGH SCHOOL students are lured into smoking the devil's lettuce by evil pushers in this 1936 film, their lives immediately spiral into melodramatic squalor and depravity. A film created during the cannabis scare that was manufactured with the enthusiastic help of William Randolph Hearst's press empire, *Reefer Madness*, subtitled "Tell Your Children," is a prime example of the propagandistic impulse that would later manifest in "very special episodes" of hit sitcoms during Reagan's turn as a drug warrior. One toke quickly snowballs into a life wasted in the gutter, as it does in a series of similar films, most notably *Marihuana* and *The Cocaine Fiends*. The year after *Reefer Madness* was released, federal prohibition of cannabis went into effect.

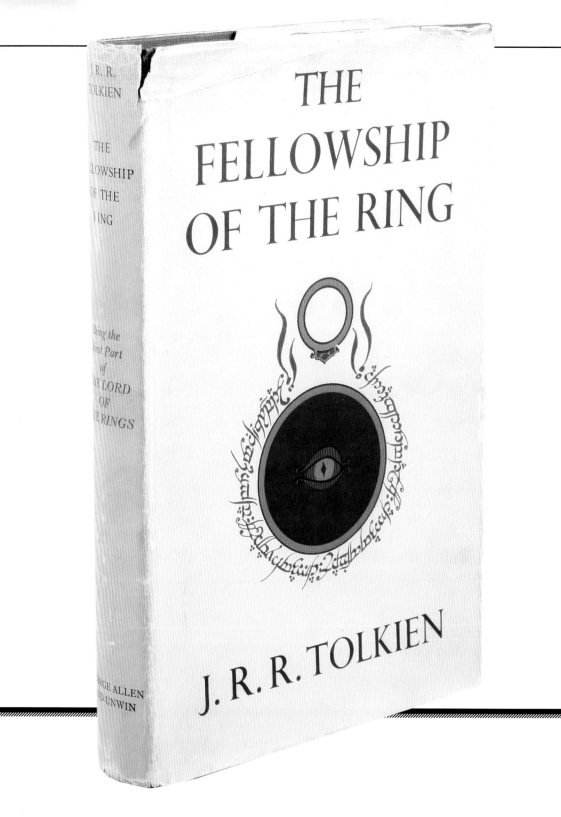

73

THE LORD OF THE RINGS

CANNABIS'S TENTATIVE STEPS during the 20th century toward mainstream acceptance can be a difficult journey to measure. Like a cloud of smoke, the source of weed's tolerance (and in some cases embrace) by the vast swath of Americans seems to have spread across the country without any one identifiable origin. But one of the sure ways we have of gauging cannabis's popularity is by examining how often it crops up in places where it's least expected—such as in discussions surrounding an epic fantasy tome written by a geriatric Oxford professor. John Ronald Reuel Tolkien's *The Lord of the Rings* (which was first published in 1954 and has since sold more than 100 million copies) presents readers with a wildly imaginative world filled with dragons, dwarves, dark lords and a diminutive race known as Hobbits, who love nothing more than a smoke of "pipe-weed" followed by a good meal. Although Tolkien never explicitly stated "pipe-weed is Middle-earth's cannabis," legions of fans quickly connected the dots between the two, and Tolkien's masterpiece has become an undeniable part of cannabis culture ever since.

WOODSTOCK PASS

WHEN THOUSANDS OF hippies descended on Max Yasgur's farm in the town of Woodstock, New York, in 1969, it was the biggest demonstration that had ever been held by the "counter-culture." It also happened to be the most epic drug-fueled rock & roll marathon the world had ever seen. Though the brown acid was famously bad stuff, the leafy green flowed like wine, and at Woodstock the wine flowed plenty. Acts and fans alike were awash in cannabis for the duration of the festival. *The New York Times* reported at the time that they estimated no less than 99 percent of the crowd was smoking as they listened to the likes of The Band, Santana, Joe Cocker, The Who, Janis Joplin, Jimi Hendrix and dozens of others.

e Menu,*
: Open.

*At Participating Castles

WHITE CASTLE "SLIDER"

IN 2004, one of the most iconic munchie-menu items in the world was elevated to near mythic status by two hapless stoner characters named Harold Lee and Kumar Patel. The Hoboken, New Jersey, natives just trying to satisfy their craving led viewers on a Homer-worthy odyssey through the Garden State that would become so popular it spawned two sequels and reinvigorated the brand that gave us the original fast food hamburger, known since its inception as "the slider." The popularity of *Harold & Kumar Go To White Castle* is based on a simple truth: When White Castle is what you crave—usually after a healthy puff of green—nothing else will suffice.

76

KAYA

IN ADDITION TO being the album that gave the world "Is This Love?" and "Satisfy My Soul," two of Bob Marley and the Wailers' smoothest and most lasting hits, *Kaya* is also Rastafari slang for cannabis. Fans have been reading the album as an extended love letter to the Wailers' favorite herb since its release in 1978. Lyrics like "Excuse me while I light my spliff, good God I gotta take a lift" from "Easy Skanking" do little to discourage these readings, but Marley's open talk of cannabis use was always part of a larger philosophy he hoped to embody. Themes of community and the similarity of all people are always part and parcel with the Wailers' message, and cannabis was simply one part of the bountiful life Marley hoped to share.

POSTER FOR CHEECH & CHONG'S *UP IN SMOKE*

STONER COMEDIES are a staple subgenre for moviegoers hoping to split their sides, but it wasn't always so. Before 1978 saw the release of Cheech and Chong's *Up In Smoke*, stoners were relegated to the fringes of film at best. The days of *Reefer Madness* might have been over, but before Cheech and Chong there had never been a stoner protagonist in a major motion picture before. *Up in Smoke* gave us two, and they went on to define cannabis-themed comedy for decades. Without *Up in Smoke*, there could be no *Super Troopers*, no *Harold and Kumar*, no *Pineapple Express*, no *Your Highness* or a dozen other comedies that shamelessly derive their yuks from the antics of those under the influence.

A LOU ADLER PRODUCTION
CHEECH & CHONG'S
Up in Smoke
HEECH MARIN AND TOMMY CHONG
ERRITT EDIE ADAMS STROTHER MARTIN AND
EACH AS SGT. STEDENKO
TOMMY CHONG & CHEECH MARIN
BY LOU ADLER & LOU LOMBARDO
Y LOU ADLER PANAVISION®
ale on Warner Bros. Records and Tapes.
Don't go straight to see this movie!
780116

UP IN SMOKE

78

THE DUDE'S RUG

"That rug really tied the room together."
—Jeff "The Dude" Lebowski,
several times

VERY SHORTLY AFTER the Coen Brothers' 1998 neo-noir comedy *The Big Lebowski* begins, the main character, named Jeffrey Lebowski but known only as The Dude (or Duder, his Dudeness or El Duderino, if you're not into the whole brevity thing), watches his rug being soiled by one of two goons who have broken into his apartment. That rug, which everyone agrees tied the whole room together, is the Macguffin in a stoner adventure that has been often imitated but never matched. The Dude, a dyed-in-the-wool 1970s radical and enthusiastic pothead, finds himself in the middle of a hardboiled mystery that would make Humphrey Bogart proud. The classic fish out of water story played out with film noir rules underperformed at the box office, but has since been recognized as a masterpiece, particularly of stoner cinema. But that's just, like, our opnion, man.

DR. DRE'S
THE CHRONIC

HIP-HOP AND CANNABIS have enjoyed a fruitful relationship since the beginning of the musical genre at smoke-wreathed house parties in the Bronx, but the official marriage between the cultural phenomenon and the leafy green can be traced to one place—the 1992 release of Dr. Dre's solo debut, *The Chronic*. Named after West Coast slang for particularly good cannabis, the record is still widely considered the best-produced hip-hop album ever. But its biggest contribution to both cannabis culture and hip-hop was introducing the world to a young Long Beach rapper who went by the stage name Snoop Dogg. Perhaps the world's most famous cannabis user and advocate, Snoop even has his own line of cannabis products called Leafs By Snoop. None of his entrepreneurship, ubiquity or frontline presence in making cannabis mainstream would have been possible without Dre's foresight in bringing the young rapper in on his *Chronic* project.

PLANTLIFE SOCKS

FROM FLAGS to T-shirts to bumper stickers, the cannabis leaf symbol—usually a sativa leaf against a colored background—has been the single most recognizable symbol in cannabis culture. But because not every cannabis user necessarily wants to step out in an I *pot leaf* NY shirt, HUF Apparel made a bestselling addition to the tradition in the 2010s that's a little more usable with everyday work attire. Called "plantlife" socks and available where HUF products are sold, the colorful tributes to weed culture are a statement without being an advertisement to be stopped and frisked.

81

THE TABLE IN FORMAN'S BASEMENT

"The oil companies control everything. Like there's this guy who invented this car that runs on water, man. It's got a fiberglass, air-cooled engine, and it runs on water, man!"
—*Steven Hyde, "That '70s Pilot"*

PREMIERING IN 1998, *That '70s Show* provided a nostalgic kickback to the 1970s for eight seasons. Following a group of suburban teens in the fictional town of Point Place, Wisconsin, from 1976 to 1979, the sitcom's themes were true to the decade—dealing with issues like equality for women, sexuality, the 1970s recession and generational conflict. Of course, a show about teenagers with "not a thing to do" in the '70s would not have been complete without touching on the popularity of pot. The characters often secretly smoked weed in Eric Forman's basement sitting around a table. "The Circle" smoking scenes are marked by the camera spinning in the middle of the table to each individual character as they speak in a thick cloud of smoke. While these scenes make audiences feel like they're also a part of Forman's puff and pass circle, the table in the basement was a concept created to comply with guidelines regarding cannabis use on TV. The table provided the perfect centerpiece for showing the gang stoned, without ever showing them physically smoking. The Circle proved to be one of the series' most beloved features, constantly churning out hilarious, nonsensical and—in Hyde's case—conspiracy riddled one-liners that are all too familiar to real pot-smokers.

82

BONGOS

"What's wrong with beating on your drums in your birthday suit? I have no regrets about the way I got there."
—**Matthew McConaughey, in an interview with** *Playboy*

BONGOS HAVE BEEN a staple of Cuban music since the late 19th century when they evolved as an offshoot of the conga drum. They have also been a staple of beat culture since the 1950s, and until 1999 the most recognizable archetype of the beatnik was clad in black, puffing on a joint and sitting cross-legged, bongos resting on the legs. But cannabis culture and bongos became even more intertwined when just before the turn of the millennium, A-lister Matthew McConaughey received a visit from the authorities after a neighbor complained of loud noises. What they heard was McConaughey, bong freshly smoked, banging a set of bongos and yelling—naked as a baby. The actor received a $50 fine for disturbing the peace and the eternal respect of anyone who's ever smoked a J and felt like banging a drum.

WEEDOPOLY

THOUGH THERE ARE dozens of
sponsored versions of Monopoly, from game
boards based on sports teams and world cities
to those based on pop culture phenomena
like Pokémon and *Star Wars*, Weedopoly
lacks a rebranded Boardwalk or Park Place
or anything else to link the cannabis board
game to the Parker Brothers classic that
inspired its name. Weedopoly, trademarked
in 2015, is a no-smoking-required (but not
discouraged either) 18 x 18 board game
that sees players "Start at Start and End
at Stoned." "Take a Hit" cards slow the
process down, while baggies of "Luck"
move your Sorry!-style game pieces
ahead. First one to "stoned" wins.

ROBERT MITCHUM'S POLICE RECORD

WHILE ACTOR ROBERT MITCHUM is best known for starring opposite Hollywood Golden Age actresses such as Ava Gardner, Marilyn Monroe and Rita Hayworth, it was his arrest for marijuana possession that made him a household name. On August 31, 1948, Mitchum, along with actress Lila Leeds and two other friends, were busted smoking pot during a police raid at Leeds's home in the Hollywood Hills. The intense media coverage lasted for months because of how shocking the story was to contemporary readers. Public perception dictated that marijuana was an illegal drug only used by minorities or those considered low class—and Mitchum was neither.

Although Mitchum and Leeds were convinced the drug bust was a setup, they were both found guilty of criminal possession and spent 60 days in jail. It was later revealed by Sgt. A.M. Barr of the LAPD that Mitchum's suspicions were true—the actor was targeted by police as a way to promote their anti-drug program. Barr told the *LA Times*, "We don't care who we have to arrest. There's a lot of 'stuff' being used in Hollywood. We have a number of important and prominent Hollywood screen personalities under surveillance."

Leeds would try and capitalize on her arrest with a *Reefer Madness*-inspired film called *She Shoulda Said "No"!* that was semi-biographical, but ultimately the drug charge ruined her career. The exposure only broadened Mitchum's appeal, however, and he was instantly rebranded as a Hollywood bad boy—he starred in award-winning films until he died in 1997.

A hybrid strain, consisting of both indica and sativa components, Blue Magoo is one of many varieties that can be found at legal dispensaries like Sticky Buds in Denver.

Miracle-Gro®

Quick Start®

Planting & Transplant Starting Solution

Solución para empezar a sembrar y trasplantar

Gives Transplants The Nutrients They Need To Thrive!

¡Proporciona a los trasplantes los nutrientes que necesitan para crecer con vigor!

Stimulates Root Growth For Faster Blooms*

Estimula el crecimiento de las raíces para obtener una floración más rápida*

Mix With Water
Se mezcla con agua

*vs Unfed Plants
*Comparado con plantas sin fertilizar

MIRACLE-GRO

THE SCOTTS Miracle-Gro company began selling lawn seed in 1868. Since then, they've become the leading brand for do-it-yourself gardeners of all kinds, from tomato planters to pot-preneurs. While their products all contribute to plant growth, during the Great Recession beginning in 2008, there was ironically no growth at the company itself. It wasn't until CEO Jim Hagedorn walked into an independent garden center in 2013 and discovered his company could target a new type of customer—cannabis growers— that business began to boom once more. Alongside rows of hydroponic equipment, he told *Forbes* in 2016 that cultivating cannabis "is the biggest thing I've seen in lawn and garden."

In 2015 Scotts Miracle-Gro invested in two companies—one in California and the other in Amsterdam—that specialized in making hydroponics equipment, lighting and accessories for pot growers. This new market was controversial for some board members at Miracle-Gro, and a few stepped down in the process. This didn't stop Hagedorn. On April 20, 2016, the company debuted a new line called "Black Magic" specifically for growing weed. Providing base nutrients, fertilizer, growing pots and supplements, the Black Magic website also provides an education guide for beginner "gardeners."

86

SPACE BUCKET

FOR MUCH OF the cannabis-using world, growing one's own crop remains a dream too risky to actually set into motion in the real world. Visions of pot farming remain just that: visions. Enter the space bucket. It's not quite enough to give you a farmerly harvest of your own, but it'll keep a single plant alive and produce sticky green with minumum effort. With a fan, a grow light, a drywall bucket and a power strip, horticulturalists strapped for space can still create a self-sustaining stash.

87

GROW LIGHT

EVER SINCE the first French research paper concerned with the possibility of growing plants by electric light, 1861's *Production de la Matiére verte des feuilles sous l'influence de la lumière éléctrique*, the horticultural world has been fascinated by the idea of growing plants by artificial light, negating the sun in its dictation of when crops could get light. Plant lighting followed a similar trajectory to lights meant for human comfort and convenience, with the two advancing in tandem until the German company Siemens studied the use of carbon arc lighting, which had a single focus point and a broad blue spectrum. Edison's incandescent bulb provided the next industry-changing standard and would power grow lights until the 1990s, when the first LED lights were developed. These "light emitting diodes" changed the way every plant could be grown, especially cannabis. While a bean farmer may benefit from lights, cannabis growers often have no other choice but to do their farming under the radar—i.e., indoors at the very least.

88

ISO SHIPPING CONTAINER

THE INTERLOCKING SHIPPING container, fixture of docksides, freight trains and the occasional action movie or video game, is the result of the inspiration and determination of a truck driver named Malcolm McLean. McLean waited an inordinate amount of time one day in 1937 for his haul to be unloaded crate by crate, carried onto a ship one by one and then waited for new cargo to be loaded one by one, and so on. The stackable rectangular ISO shipping container was inspired that monotonous day, but McLean would have to build himself from trucker to trucking company owner before he had the commercial muscle to do anything about his idea. Once his container was introduced, it became the standard for international and bulk shipping—which also made it one of the go-tos for international smuggling. The cannabis industry got its fair share of use out of the container's traditional purpose, but ISO shipping containers are also big enough, as enterprising DIY homeowners would discover in the 2010s, to support a small house, office or even a mom and pop grow operation.

CANNABIS CUP

COMIC BOOK FANS have Comic Con, Disney fans have D23, Juggalos have the Gathering and pot enthusiasts have the Cannabis Cup. A convention the likes of which would be completely foreign to denizens of the corporate world, the Cup refers to both the gathering and the grand prize given to the strains that have stolen the show every year since 1988, when *High Times* founded it. Now a traveling expo that awards multiple categories in multiple cities throughout the course of the year, the Cannabis Cup is where the world's top potrepreneurs gather to forge the future of weed. They're also always great collections of cannabis culture's finest art, artists and scientists.

Skunk is a strain that was first produced in the 1980s, based on the so-called land race strains—naturally growing cannabis like Acapulco Gold and Durban Poison.

90

CANNABIS BATH SOAK

ONE OF THE most interesting implications of the newly legal status of cannabis in many U.S. states is that smoking and eating are no longer the only ways users can experiment with the plant. For example, those suffering from sore muscles or joint pain might find relief in one of Dixie Elixirs' bath products, which can be added to a piping hot tub to release THC directly into the bathwater. The perfect combination of the effects of an edible and the strongest cup of sleepytime tea you've ever had, a cannabis-infused bath is being recognized by longtime enthusiasts and first time users alike as the ideal introduction to cannabis.

91

FORIA OIL

SINCE ANCIENT near-eastern and subcontinental cultures began burning cannabis flowers for the effect, one of the most commonly appreciated—but not necessarily talked about—aspects of cannabis has been its use as an aphrodisiac. For centuries, the bedroom potential of the plant was associated with the quasi-intimate experience of sharing a bowl or joint with someone as well as the anecdotally accepted but not clinically proven idea that a cannabis high simply makes sex feel better. Shortly after legalization for recreational purposes got its start in 2013, a company called Foria sought to take what was nebulous and make it concrete by introducing the first THC-infused sex product. When Foria, a topical rub meant to increase sensitivity for women, hit the market it was lauded by *GQ* as the "sex-product of the year" thanks to THC's tingling effects, sure to be appreciated by both parties in an amorous and perhaps smoke-wreathed tryst.

92

PROPOSITION 502

SIXTEEN YEARS after California first legalized medical cannabis, Washington placed Proposition 502 on its 2012 ballot. The measure—which would go on to pass—made recreational use of cannabis legal for adults over the age of 21, making Washington, along with Colorado, which passed a similar resolution around the same time, the first states to legalize the recreational use of cannabis since the 1930s. In its first two years of legal sales, Washington topped more than $1 billion in tax revenue for the state, making it a formidable cash crop and job creator.

IN THE EVERG...

est. 2012

Farmer J's
Established 2013
"The Green Standard"
Sour Kush
Net weight: 2 grams
Lot/Batch:000 0149 Harvested: 8/18/14 Tested: 6/29/14

20.4%	<.01%	<.01%
THC-Total	CBD-Total	CBG-Total

THC-Acid 17.9%	CBD-Acid< 01%	CBG-Acid< 01%
THC-dcrb 2.47%	CBD-dcrb< 01%	CBG-dcrb< 01%
Total Cannabinoid	20.4%	CBN: <.01%
Active Cannabinoid	2.47%	THC8: <.01%

Tested by Confidence Analytics   farmerjs.com

Compliant with CA Prop 215 SB 420

Medical Cannabis

COMPASSIONATE USE ACT-COMPLIANT MEDS

WHEN CALIFORNIANS became the first citizens of the U.S. to pass a law allowing medical cannabis, it was the first step in a march that is still ongoing, albeit at a faster pace now than ever. The "Compassionate Use Act" was a fairly simple referendum. It consisted of three statements and a provision allowing for the law's repeal. As the first medical cannabis legislation in the country, it's worth including the three statements here:

"[Proposition 215] Exempts patients and defined caregivers who possess or cultivate marijuana for medical treatment recommended by a physician from criminal laws which otherwise prohibit possession or cultivation of marijuana; Provides physicians who recommend use of marijuana for medical treatment shall not be punished or denied any right or privilege; Declares that measure not be construed to supersede prohibitions of conduct endangering others or to condone diversion of marijuana for nonmedical purposes." From 1996 on, California stood as the first state to defy federal law on cannabis, thanks to pill bottles like the one pictured, the three statements above and millions of votes in favor of them.

GUMMIES

IN JUNE 2016, Colorado Gov. John Hickenlooper, the same governor who had presided over the state's transition to the first legal cannabis zone in the country, signed a bill into law that would make one of the most popular—and controversial—products in the new cannabis market illegal again. Cannabis gummy bears, each infused with roughly 10mg of cannabis, had been a point of concern for Coloradans since the 2012 vote that allowed for legalization. Identical to normal gummy candies in every way except their packaging, fears that they would attract underage users proved too strong to ignore. While gummies are still available in some states, they are also the most consistently decried cannabis product in legal states.

THE VIENNA DIOSCORIDES

A CODEX DATED from the early 6th century A.D., the Vienna Dioscorides is the earliest manuscript we have concerning the sciences of botany and horticulture. The codex is a 512 A.D. Byzantine copy of a work by Roman surgeon Pedanius Dioscorides, who compiled the uses for hundreds of plants and herbs as he traveled with Emperor Nero's legions in the first century. Dioscorides's work is the first medical mention of the cannabis plant we have, dating from the Western Roman Empire and proving that the West knew of and utilized cannabis for its medicinal properties in the ancient world, as did its Eastern counterparts.

96

PATENT MEDICINE

DURING THE 19th century, the market for so-called patent medicines was booming. Cannabis was a common ingredient in some of these, but they were often laced with much stronger compounds like morphine and cocaine. Patent medicines were sold as miracle cures because they often made the patient feel much, much better.

But they weren't cured, just very high. When the Harrison Act was introduced in 1914, it was to crack down on the morphine and cocaine making fiends out of well-meaning people all over the country, but cannabis was caught in the hard-drug crossfire for the first time thanks to the patent medicine industry.

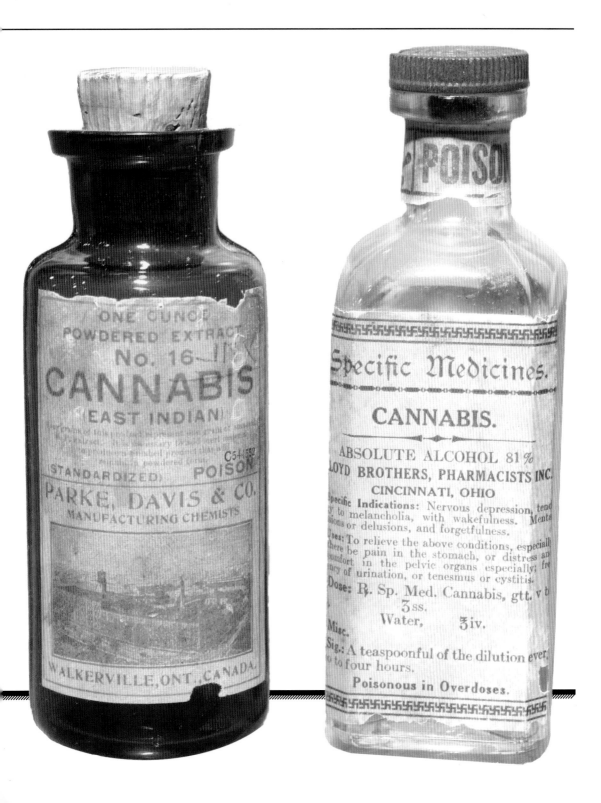

97

MEDICAL CANNABIS CARD

FOR PATIENTS in states that allow the use of their medicine, the Cannabis Card is just as important as the driver's license or government I.D. Without it, they are criminals every time they take their prescribed dose. With it, they are able to walk into a store, lay their money on the counter and walk out with the finest green bud money can buy. For a host of patients with just as many painful conditions, the Medical Cannabis Card is a lifeline. What would have been viewed as an impossibility along the lines of a "Get out of jail free card" just a few decades ago is now normal in more than 20 states.

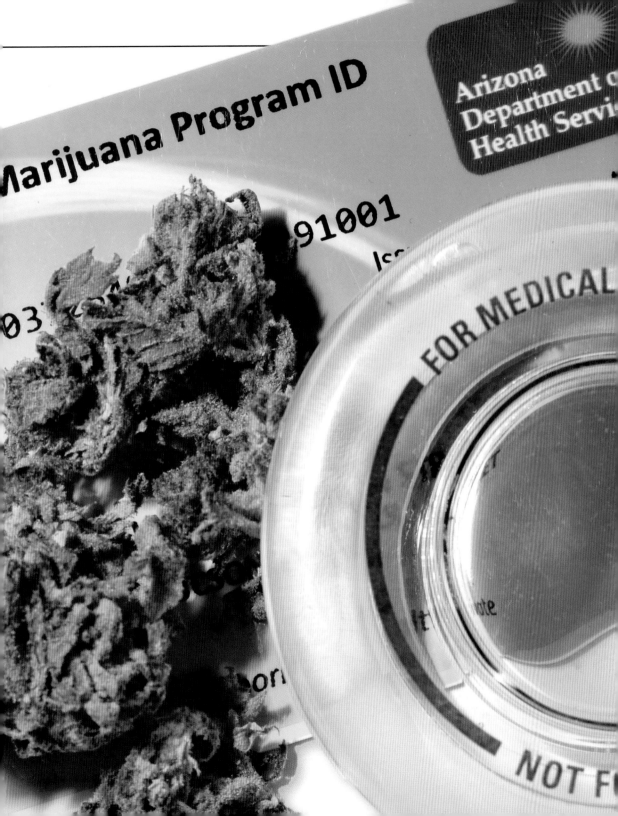

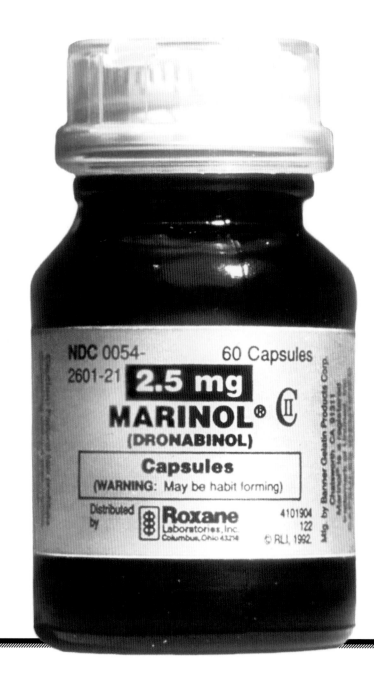

98

MARINOL

ONE OF THE MOST well-known and fondly mocked side effects of cannabis is that it often leads to a sudden and nagging hunger. While this may result in unwanted growing waistlines of many cannabis users, for chemotherapy patients, it turns out that the munchies is often the main reason for trying cannabis in the first place. An effective counter against the crippling nausea induced by chemo, cannabis not only stops one feeling queasy, but also gives a much-needed hunger pang to those for whom mealtimes are less a pleasure than a chore. For this reason, it is also given to those suffering weight loss from HIV/AIDS complications. Marinol is cannabis's original pharmaceutical cousin, administered by a doctor from a branded medicine bottle in sterile confines—a treatment not even the most draconian drug warrior could argue with.

99

CBD OIL

OIL-BASED CANNABIS extracts focused on CBD, a non-psychoactive component of the flower, have proved so useful in treating epileptic illnesses that even bastions of Bible Belt conservatism like Alabama have allowed for its use in the confines of their otherwise cannabis-unfriendly state. Beginning in 2012 with the study "Cannabinoids for Epilepsy," the floodgates have weakened and eventually broken, proving that CBD is effective in a majority of cases in which those with epileptic conditions did not respond to traditional treatments.

REAL SCIENT

HEMP O

[RSHO

^CBD Liquid: F

1000mg Cannabidi

4 fl oz (120ml)

100

LEAFS
BY SNOOP

WHEN SNOOP DOGG, both one of the world's biggest rappers and perhaps the highest-profile cannabis user anywhere, announced in 2015 that he would have his own brand of cannabis products, few people were surprised. In fact, many were excited to have their stash curated by and bearing the name of a cannabis legend.

The Leafs website offers this message from Snoop himself: "Wherever my musical journey has taken me around the world, it's beautiful to see how chronic leafs are a common source of peace, love and soul that connects us all. I've always been proud of our movement and have personally selected my favorite strains to enjoy. Leafs by Snoop is my way of sharing the experience I have with the finest quality cannabis one could imagine."

101

MBOX

THE SUBSCRIPTION SERVICE, whether it's for comic book lovers, dog owners, golfers, grillers or cigar aficionados, is a staple of our online, on-demand culture. It offers three things that are irresistible to the American consumer: specialized gadgets and trinkets, our favorite hobbies and the ability to have both delivered directly to us with minimal effort. So it's no surprise that one of the most successful up-and-coming subscription services is MBox, sending subscribing stoners a monthly care package of specially curated buds, concentrates and cannabis-themed merchandise. Available to Californians, MBox offers a $200 value of the finest cannabis for $97/month.